EMERGING

EMERGING

A Pilsdon Diary

❖❖❖❖❖❖❖❖❖❖❖❖❖❖❖❖❖❖❖

NIGEL CAPON

CAIRNS PUBLICATIONS
HARLECH
2003

British Library Cataloguing in Publication Data.
A record for this book is available from the British Library.

Every effort has been made to acknowledge copyright material.
Any omissions will be corrected at the earliest opportunity.
Acknowledgements are made as follows:

The Tao of Pooh and the Te of Piglet Copyright © 1982, 1992, 1994, 1998
and 2002 by Benjamin Hoff, published by Egmont Books Ltd.

Peter Pan: The Story of Lost Childhood, Kathleen Kelley-Lainé.
Copyright © 1997 Element Books Ltd. Text © 1992 Calmann-Lévy.

ISBN 1 870652 39 8

CAIRNS PUBLICATIONS
Dwylan, Stryd Fawr, Harlech, Gwynedd LL46 2YA

www.cottercairns.co.uk
office@cottercairns.co.uk – orders
jim@cottercairns.co.uk – editorial

Typeset in Monotype Columbus by
Strathmore Publishing Services, London EC1

Printed in Great Britain by
Stanley L. Hunt, Rushden

CONTENTS

LIST OF PHOTOGRAPHS

A NOTE ON TREES

How many trees have been used to publish this book? Well, only the pulp is used, which comes from the trimmings: the trunks are used for furniture. A commercially grown soft wood tree produces, on average, about one-sixth of a ton of pulp. Since this book has used about one ton, it has needed six trees to produce it – but of course not all of those six trees. By weight it has needed about three-quarters of one tree. So Cairns Publications is donating the wherewithal for the planting of two trees, in gratitude and recompense.

FOREWORD

THE REVD PETER BARNETT

Warden of the Pilsdon Community from 1994

Many words have been written, spoken and preached about the Pilsdon Community, but to my knowledge no one has published their experiences and reflections on being a guest at Pilsdon. Keeping a journal during his stay at Pilsdon is part of his healing journey and I am very indebted to Nigel Capon for having the fortitude and courage now to produce it to be published.

Nigel, like many thousand others during the last forty-three years, came to Pilsdon in a state of crisis and breakdown. He came not knowing what to expect. So the first lesson I have learnt from this diary is the importance of that initial contact and journey by car from Crewkerne railway station or Bridport coach station to Pilsdon. The conversation and description of life at Pilsdon are crucial to allay initial fears and facilitate settling into our community life.

I also learnt from this diary how important the 'Barnabas Ministry' is in healing and recovery. What I mean by this is the various ways you can encourage people. Whether that be by not taking them for granted, or noticing and encouraging the small routine tasks and chores in daily living, or suggesting ways that can draw out a person's skills and creativity (in Nigel's case music making and composing) and so build up their confidence and self-esteem.

By not censoring the descriptions of his feelings, Nigel takes us into the much-misunderstood area of depression.

This is an important contribution to a state of life that affects increasingly more people, as isolation in our hectic society becomes more common. I hope those who read this diary will be helped to understand the incapacitating nature of depression and how the best help for the sufferer is often just to know and be assured that friends are there and that the sufferer is loved. Words are often the least important response, it is one's presence and availability. Community life has that quality built into it, in contrast to the isolation of independent living. This presence and availability is also related to our relationship with God, which in depression can seem absent, but for some can be a 'dark night of the soul' which later becomes a spiritually deepening time.

   In this diary we get a picture of community life from a new perspective – that of someone who wanted to contribute to the life of the community but sometimes found that physically, mentally, and emotionally he could not. Nigel came to Pilsdon in a state of 'breakdown'. While living at Pilsdon he 'broke down'. Nigel found that Pilsdon was a safe place to break down and rebuild at a manageable pace. Nigel has said: "The 'stiff-upper-lip' syndrome which had bogged my life for years, seemed to drift away – maybe reflecting a quality in the environment which exists at Pilsdon, which is not often noticed." Also, when he decided to move on to independent living, he found that was not always easy and so he has kept close links with Pilsdon. I think this begins to give some direction to the concept of 'living alongside a community'.

   When I was reading Nigel's diary I couldn't help comparing some of it with Jim Cotter's book, *Brainsquall,** where he describes his time of depression and recovery with his friends. I am grateful to Nigel for 'baring his soul' in this diary. I hope it

---

* Jim Cotter, *Brainsquall: soundings from a deep depression*, Cairns Publications in association with Arthur James, 1997.

encourages others to use the writing of a journal as a means of seeking wholeness and holiness in life. I also hope that it encourages people to seek out Christian communities (particularly if you don't have the support of family or friends) as places where one's spiritual journey can be encouraged, no matter how much in the depths you might feel.

Feast of the Transfiguration of Christ, 2001

Welcome to Pilsdon

ACKNOWLEDGEMENTS

To Peter, the warden, and his wife Mary – a heartfelt thank you for your love, care, support, and advice, especially during those darkest moments.

To Andrew, Alan, Anthony, Sandra and Chris, Jonathan and Suzie, all members of the community during my stay at Pilsdon – thank you for making time for me, for your love and care and patience.

To the volunteers at Pilsdon who also made time for me and listened – especially Oliver, Sarah and Alex, and Emily – thank you. To all residents, visitors and wayfarers who befriended me during my stay – thank you.

To Othona at Burton Bradstock, especially Tony, thank you for your love, help, and beautiful spaces for relaxation, meditation, inspiration, and creativity.

To Brother Aidan and Brother Sam, a sincere thank you for your love and spiritual strength and comfort during my various stays at Hilfield Friary.

A special thank you to Mike, my advocate, who helped me so much while I was in a turmoil about things.

Thank you to Rahel Hoffmann for her beautiful photo of the sunrise over Marshwood Vale with one of my favourite trees, which has been used on the cover.

NIGEL CAPON
March 2003

Community life at Pilsdon

PILSDON COMMUNITY

Pilsdon is a working community, and those people staying there work according to their abilities, helping with domestic chores, preparing fruit and vegetables etc. for meals, cooking, washing and drying up, maintenance of the house and out-buildings etc., care for the animals – sheep, cows, pigs, chickens and hens and ducks, donkeys and Daisy the goat – and looking after the dairy or the flower and vegetable gardens.

Pilsdon offers a refuge for people who are seeking respite from the stresses of everyday life – it is a place where people are able to work through depression, alcoholism, drug addiction, divorce, or bereavement. It is a place for recuperation. Pilsdon helps people to heal, to rebuild their lives, enabling them to look forward to a brighter future.

Worship and spirituality are at heart Anglican, but people of any faith, or none, of any race or culture, are made welcome.

Pilsdon offers a therapeutic environment of communal living and manual work, with creative opportunities – pottery, art crafts, music, recreation – and pastoral care.

All proceeds from the sale of this book go to the Pilsdon Community. If you would like to know more and/or make a donation please write to:

The Warden, The Pilsdon Community, Pilsdon Manor, Pilsdon, Bridport, Dorset, DT6 5NZ

Tel: 01308 868308
Fax: 01308 868161
E-mail: pilsdon@lineone.net
Web site: http//website.lineone.net/~pilsdon

Psalm 13

How long, O Lord? Will you forget me for ever?
How long will you hide your face from me?
How long must I wrestle with my thoughts
And every day have sorrow in my heart?
How long will my enemy triumph over me?

Look on me and answer, O Lord my God.
Give light to my eyes, or I will sleep in death;
My enemy will say, 'I have overcome him',
And my foes will rejoice when I fall.

But I trust in your unfailing love;
My heart rejoices in your salvation;
I will sing to the Lord,
For he has been good to me.

PROLOGUE

It was during the course of just eleven months that I lived through a number of events which caused me mental and emotional breakdown.

First of all I moved house and then became engaged – continually attending the Royal London Hospital for tests and examinations. I then moved house again and became married – still attending the hospital every week – and then moved house again and had more medical tests. I was then mugged, and went on sick leave having become mentally ill – hearing voices and suffering hallucinations – and then had an operation on the groin after which I became separated from my wife and once again moved house. While all this was going on I was grieving over the loss of a couple of very dear friends whom I loved dearly.

On the advice of friends and wife, and the Association for Pastoral Retreats, I came to Pilsdon in September 1995. I felt suicidal, mentally and emotionally all over the place; weak, helpless, fragile, tired, and exhausted. Everything black – I felt I was in a tunnel – in an abyss.

Pilsdon opened me up to suppressed feelings and emotions, hurts and pains – but gradually I began to feel someone of worth – finding the true inner self. And the healing process began. After years and years of putting on an act, I had lost who I really was. Not only putting on an act, but being someone everybody else wanted me to be – keeping my true self inside an inner shell; suppressing feelings with a stiff upper lip learnt through patterns of behaviour that began early in childhood.

Pilsdon Community from the air

Most, if not all, of my adult life had been materialistic; not allowing myself time for spiritual growth.

What follows is an account taken from a diary I kept every day for the first few months of my stay at Pilsdon, and records what I was going through at the time, and how Pilsdon became the catalyst for a change in my life and helped set about the beginnings of a holistic healing process.

There are a lot of swear words which appear in the diary as I wrote it during my stay at Pilsdon. I decided to keep the whole lot in, to give some idea of what it was really like for me at the time. I hope that this doesn't upset the reader too much.

SHORT VISIT

Monday 11 September 1995
Left on bus to go to Chelmsford. Angry – tearful – anxious –
feel that everybody's watching me: want them all to go away –
too many people – want to be alone – want to die – feel
confused – what the fuck am I doing? Feel tired – exhausted –
hearing voices again, and seeing black shadows behind me –
want to fight. Feels like a whirlwind inside me; so many things,
feelings, memories and thoughts, whirling around and around
and around.

On the train to Crewkerne. What's Pilsdon like? Who's
there? Nervous apprehension. Tried to distract myself by doing
a crossword – no good, can't concentrate. Looked out of the
window, didn't notice anything really – nothingness – a blank
– just want to curl up and sleep.

Crewkerne. Anxiety levels up – sweating a lot – shaking.
Who's meeting me? Drove to Pilsdon with Mary and her
children, who had been blackberry picking. Felt calmer. Was
shown around on arrival. And spent some time with the pigs
for some reason. Lovely gardens – otherwise I don't think I
noticed very much.

Supper. Nervous again – felt like a kid back at boarding
school. Will I fit in? Who are all these people? What is
expected of me? Want to be alone.

Tuesday 12 September
Morning. Didn't sleep – too much whirling around – voices
troubling me again, wish they would go away. Feel cold – went
to morning prayer and felt a little calmer afterwards. Did the

washing-up after breakfast and felt OK about that. During the rest of the morning did some more domestic chores – I still want to be alone – don't fit in – this is not the place for me; but then where is?

I feel there's a whirlwind inside me – it's all too much – too much for me to cope with – the bloody pains that brought me to all this – I feel I have nothing – don't feel wanted – just want to go home; but where the fuck is home?

Feel like shit.

Feel's as if there's a knot in my stomach – someone's in there, or something is twisting it tighter and tighter and tighter.

While I'm writing this diary I'm beginning to feel just a little calmer, less shaking and tremors and less sweating – but somehow I feel I've had enough – feel out in the cold – no warmth – just want to disappear.

Afternoon. Spent some time with the pigs – suddenly I feel a bit better about being here! Feelings fluctuating from one thing to another – there's so much stuff to work through – maybe Pilsdon is the place to do this: but I don't really know. Why do I want to be alone so much? UGH!

There's so much come up from this just one very short visit – it's going to take an awful lot of effort to go through it all: it's all so daunting – and now I am reminded of memories of boarding school again. I keep on having those since arriving here. There are some ghastly memories relating to sexual abuse which disturb me a lot. I had forgotten all about it over the years until now. Oh well – it's just the great big mound of things that are whirling around: if only I could push it all away! But I suppose I should have a little bit of courage, and experience 'the going through it' – the memories are all part of my life – in fact a big part.

If I could just find some sort of role to play here just maybe

I would find things a little easier – and maybe I would just find a little bit of a sense of achievement and fulfilment. However much I want to be alone, I think there are certain times when it is unwise and unhealthy: but hopefully if I am accepted here then there may be times when I just find my own space.

Night-time. Went to Evensong – found it really difficult to concentrate, but I found it peaceful and calming. Had a good chat with Peter, and somehow felt that a decision had been reached and that Pilsdon was looking forward to my being here. I feel that now Peter knows my background and the nature of the breakdown, he is being very supportive, and any apprehension that was around has diminished. I feel OK about it all now – about being here that is. The resident who showed me around Pilsdon, including the pigs, wondered how the chat with Peter went, and when I told him he responded by saying, "Good, you're coming to stay!" I'm speechless.

Wednesday 13 September
Morning. After all that happened yesterday I would have thought I would have slept well – I didn't. I feel so angry about everything that has brought me to all this – I want to strangle someone – my wife would do for one. I feel so exhausted – I want to curl up – (in actual fact maybe I really want to go back to the warmth and security of my mother's womb) – foetal position.

Had some breakfast – ate so much – absolutely stuffed.

What made me write this journal? I don't know – but I will continue with it because it seems as if it is helping me in some way. Some sort of process has already begun during this short visit which has to continue. Suddenly, as I write this, I'm feeling that I'm being drawn to Pilsdon – I could have shut myself away and covered myself in a blanket and not let the place touch me – but I didn't. Somehow, though, I feel frightened

South view of the manor house

about what is going to come up out of my subconscious during
my next stay at Pilsdon, especially with regard to suppressed
feelings and emotions and the events that go with them.
However, a date's been fixed and I shall be coming back to
Pilsdon for a longer visit starting next Monday.

LONG VISIT

Monday 25 September
Last Thursday I moved myself and my belongings out of Essex to Surrey where my sister lives. Traumatic move – angry, tearful, and I kept on reliving the attack and mugging for some reason, seeing shadows behind me and hearing voices again – keep on telling me to kill people and kill myself.

Arrived at Pilsdon during the afternoon – Mary chatted with me about the nature of Pilsdon which helped me feel a bit better about things.

Whirling around – feel cold – feel exhausted – began to remember the train ride and standing on the edge of the platform to end things once and for all. An elderly woman saw me and came up to me and asked the time. While we talked she guided me gently back to a seat. She noticed the sadness in my eyes. She introduced herself and I told her my name and where I was going and she knew Pilsdon well, and Hilfield. We got on the train together and exchanged addresses etc.

Chatted for a while with one of the residents in the dormitory. Feeling frightened again – memories of boarding school again – UGH! – began to remember the abuses there – anxious – nervous – sweating – shaking. Took a walk round the courtyard and gardens for a while which helped. Sat down on a bench and cried – couldn't stem the flow of tears – couldn't sleep.

Wednesday 27 September
Morning. Another bad night. Feeling awkward – helped clear the sitting room for the chimney sweep after breakfast. Still

hearing voices: wish they would go away – seeing shadows – so much whirling around – feel dizzy with it all. Feel at a loss.

Afternoon. Picked some acorns for the pigs! Lots of windfalls in Peter's garden at the cottage: apparently the pigs will love them – bless them! The pigs should be transferred to the garden to wipe up the windfall apples, but they'd never get there with so many distractions like acorns around. So the acorns have to be removed from the road into sacks so that they can then be fed to the pigs at a later date. Spent some time in church after tea – felt a bit calmer – it's nice and peaceful there but my mind wasn't – if only! I wish I could just let things be for a while. I was asked if I would move to the guest loose box, which I did, wondering who I would be sharing with – felt uneasy, and a bit nervous. But once we introduced ourselves and began chatting, I began to calm down a bit – hope we get on.

*A view of the courtyard
with Pilsdon Pen in the background*

Saturday 30 September
Beginning to sleep a little better than I was – hope it lasts! – slightly less agitated – less intensity too. Seem to be getting on with the other residents OK, including the one I'm sharing the room with. He's suffering from depression – I feel for him. I do like spending time in the chapel and church – although my faith is not at all strong at the moment – indeed, even if it exists at all – I do find these two places lovely and calm and peaceful, and I do try to attend some services even so.

Beginning to do some digging in the vegetable gardens and I guess that is helping to take off a certain amount of anger which lies buried inside me – and so maybe that is also helping me to feel a bit less agitated and more calm. Also, I'm not on my own either since there is a wayfarer working with me who seems to know a lot about gardening and the soil etc. Anyway, he's a very interesting man, and we seem to get on quite well and have very interesting conversations – which is helping me to keep my mind off what is happening to me – also it's good to be out in the fresh air.

Sunday 1 October
Bloody hell – the intensity in the emotions and feelings and the whirling around and around are increasing. It's my wedding anniversary – angry – tearful – I want to knock somebody's head in – and it's bloody raining as well. Worked during the morning in the garden and got drenched – knackered – wayfarer said I was mad! It all seems so black – I'm struggling to get some light but just can't reach it somehow – there is none – it's all black and dark. Chatted with Mary which helped such a lot and cried on her shoulder and had a hug – why the fuck can't I be strong? Played some chess games during the afternoon and kept on losing but it didn't seem to matter to me – couldn't concentrate – felt I needed company – didn't want to be alone – now there's a change! Trying to read a book called

The Lost Heart of Asia by Colin Thubron and in it I've read a quote by Turcoman:

> Without knowledge of his past a man is nothing; he can't understand himself: he disappears.

Food for thought. Later on I discover that the wayfarer I was working with in the gardens has been taken to hospital – a bit of a shock – I do hope he'll be OK.

Went to the service this evening and had some supper afterwards. I met a couple of wayfarers who sat at the table where I was and they had me in fits of laughter – what a medicine! They began speaking and acting extremely poshly – all la-di-da! The things they were coming out with were absolutely hilarious – a pain in the stomach! Just when everything seemed so black, this happens. Went to bed – tired but can't sleep – memories come flooding back of the wedding – the people – the music – the party – the honeymoon. Where are my friends now? UGH!

Monday 2 October
Met with Peter – a really good chat – understanding what I was going through and he quite rightly pointed out to me that my wife was probably going through hell too. I mentioned that I played the piano. Oh no! Why don't I keep my mouth shut? Now I've let myself in for it. I was asked if I would play for a couple of hymns on Wednesday – Francis of Assisi – oh well, it'll help me feel more a part of things I guess.

Began to feel more relaxed – weather's changed – did more digging – the garden seems to have grown in size – aching all over – knackered – whirling around – dizzy with it all. Problems become insignificant compared to everyone else's – beginning to listen to other people – beginning to care about the others I've made friends with. Digging the garden is diffusing some of the anger I think – hope so – maybe it will release some of the frustrations and tensions too.

Peter Barnett

Loads of people around – lots of visitors – a bunch of schoolgirls too. Mary asked me if I wanted a hand digging the garden since I was on my own. I said that a couple of girls wouldn't go amiss. Made the tea and toast for everybody and we celebrated a guest's birthday with a gorgeous cake and some pressies too. He also got the bumps – he was nineteen.

Tuesday 3 October
Oh God – had a really upsetting phone call from my wife – and, just by the way, where is HE in all this mess? Went and did some more digging – tensions – finding it helpful somehow to be outside amongst nature. During the coffee break I went and sat in the meadow instead of sitting in the house chapel. It was a bit chilly, but it was lovely – calming and relaxing – feel less agitated – intensity died down a bit. Met up with Mary who pointed out to me that it took courage to come to a place like Pilsdon and be 'opened up' as I was allowing myself to be opened up – began to feel better about myself as I thought about what she said – returned to digging!

Turning the soil over

It occurs to me that what I am doing is turning the soil over – preparing it and nurturing it – turning things over – preparing the soil for the future. Aren't I doing the same thing by living here at Pilsdon? – preparing myself for the future? Maybe by turning things over I'm having a greater understanding of myself which I suppose is no bad thing. Spoke with Andrew for the first time really and I opened up completely – he was so patient and tolerant with me.

Friday 6 October
Finding it difficult to sleep with all these powerful emotions whirling around – memories whirling around and around – spin, spin, spin – schooldays at boarding school – deaths of family and friends – suicides at the hospital where I worked and suicides since – break up of a previous relationship in 1980 – and now all this – UGH! Played at the service last Wednesday and felt good about that – having done it I feel a sense of relief somehow. Welcomed another new guest to the loose box.

During the afternoon more digging and met Anthony – shared some thoughts about what was going on with me – it's so difficult to stand back in 'good grace' – I'm so bitter and angry about how my life has gone – but whilst I've been here, and it's been only a short while really, I believe Pilsdon has begun to 'touch me' – begun to put things in context and perspective. I do like listening to other people – the members are so helpful – I must try to remain open – don't shut myself in. When I first came here my problems were the most important thing, but gradually I am finding that others here have just as many important problems as I have. I must register with the GP.

Listened to the other guest in the loose box and I feel we'll get on OK. Began to feel nervous again – back to digging. I like attending the chapel and church services – it seems a

The interior of St Mary's Church

good way of having a quiet break from everything – especially the Services of Light on Saturday evenings in candlelight – they're lovely.

After supper Peter said he wondered who should do the washing-up. After a while in silence, and my mind was miles away, I felt a hand on my shoulder. "You don't have to say a thing," I said, "sometimes prayers help and sometimes they don't!" People laughed.

The only thing that I have difficulty with in the services is trying to find the right page so that I can follow what's going on – something to do with the lack of concentration at present I expect. There are so many times when I feel a complete and absolute idiot.

Saturday 7 October
More digging. Andrew mentioned to me that he and the other members of the community were there for me when I felt the need to talk. So much to cope with – too much – can't handle it – want it all to go away and leave me alone – feel like death – don't want to exist – had enough – it's all so dark – black – black – no light just want everything to stop. Don't notice things like I used to – moods fluctuate so much – can't concentrate – whirling around and around and around – O God, I wish it would stop.

It certainly is not an easy life here. It's like the veil of the temple being torn down to shreds and everyone seeing all the innards, all the mysteries and secrets, and seeing the whole temple for the first time. That's what it feels like to me. I'm terrified. The shell I hid behind, with all the suppressed hurts and pains, memories, feelings and emotions, and experiences in life, is all torn apart somehow. I'm beginning to find out who I really am, I think – but I must admit that most of the time at present I feel like a nobody. What hurts too are the memories of the abuse that I've dealt with in my life. Memories of the

sexual abuse at boarding school come flooding back now –
UGH!

I'm beginning to remember what Berne said about humans
carrying a burden since birth – as long as we are in the mother's
womb we are comfortable, warm and secure – we are fed and
don't do a thing for ourselves. At birth, the pain and the hurt
of being rejected from it all, is presumably too much – the cord
is cut – we become independent – we are abandoned into
another sort of life – there is also the physical pain of being
rejected from the womb and out through a 'tunnel'. The pain
and hurt lays on the shoulders of the baby who can only have
a concept of itself – it does not, when it's born, know mother
as a mother, so it blames itself for the pain and hurt that's been
caused. If in someway this applies to me, then I would see it as
a beginning of self-abuse – blaming myself for the hurt caused
by others – and so over the years I do not know any other way
to live but to continue the regime of blaming myself and abusing myself – patterns of behaviour. I need to know another way
of life – I need to learn a new pattern of behaviour. All this
whirling around of feelings, emotions, and memories of events
in my life all seem connected – one thing sparks off another –
memories of people, deaths, failures in relationships, failures in
business – it all seems never ending – one thing leads on to
another – all whirling around in a muddle – all mixed up –
can't seem to focus on any particular one thing – can't work
things through – I want it all to stop. For so long I've portrayed
a stiff upper lip – you've got to be strong, Nigel – well, fuck it,
I've had enough. Should I really stride along like a proud
soldier? Well, I've tried for what seems the majority of my life,
but now things have come to a head, so to speak. Most of my
failures have let my family down, I feel, and colleagues and
friends. I'm finding this all so difficult – can't find a way out –
I might as well end it all – I've had enough.

I don't know – one minute I'm so down in the depths of an

abyss, then the next I don't feel so bad – up and down like a bloody yo-yo – one minute I feel energized, then the next minute I feel totally exhausted.

I just wonder about the idea of the temple. If Jesus was telling us something about the veil of the temple, in that he had no defence mechanisms whatsoever and laid himself open for all to see – then if we do have faith, strength and courage, trust, loyalty and commitment, why can't we be like it too? What is it that we are having difficulty with? Is it that we possibly cannot open ourselves because we are too scared and frightened to find what's really inside? Has our culture and society provided us with something to hide behind and to use as an excuse? Are we that scared to face the God in ourselves? – because of our consciences? – guilt, perhaps, is a destroyer. Yet we who profess the faith still continue to destroy God's creation – and maybe we have so many intense hidden mysteries and secrets that there is no way we can even contemplate being open as Jesus was. Bloody hell – there's a mouthful of mish-mash – or whatever – thoughts that try to block out the reality – which I don't think is what I'm doing.

I seem to be getting on with the other guest – he's becoming something of a brother figure and father figure. I do sense some warmth though which I do find at present both comforting and reassuring. Throughout my life till now, I've been so relaxed in women's company, and have found men's company rather difficult to handle – never been relaxed in men's company: always very tense. But now I feel I'm changing.

Sunday 8 October
Although Pilsdon is a working community and there is so much going on, somehow I do feel a sense of peace here. If only I can clutch it and hold on to it. If only I could let the peace rest and dwell within me so that I could take it wherever I go. Woke up in utter agony this morning – lower abdomen

Garden maintenance

again: made me bend double. Confused before I sat down to write this about what day it was – time seems to have no particular interest for me at present. Didn't sleep at all well – have become really angry about my situation and everything – maybe that was the cause of the pain – psychological affecting the physical. Later I went for a walk up the Pen – and bloody chilly it was – glad I went though – fantastic view – and looking down on Pilsdon community it all looked so small – but when I'm there everything seems so large. Spoke with Peter about the anniversary celebrations. Would I like to play something during a short concert? Yes sure, but how about if I actually wrote something? Like a Pastorale? So the conversation went something like that. So I have now got some time off doing chores, mainly in the afternoon, in order to spend time composing.

Wednesday 11 October
Since arriving here I find that now I'm really appreciating the conversations and chats with the members, and what has come out of them mainly is that I must not push myself. In actual fact, because the issues I'm facing are so numerous and in depth, while I'm here at Pilsdon I may not resolve any of the problems, but maybe, with Pilsdon's help, I will be able to cope with them better than I am at the moment, and change my attitude towards them. I can't possibly change history – but maybe while I'm here I can also change my attitude towards myself, and find out who the real me is.

So, during the last couple of days I have spent my time between digging and composing and writing out my version of the 'Sicilienne' by Theresa von Paradis for cello and piano – I have an organ arrangement, but it was originally written for cello and piano – and since I'm gradually getting to know a cellist who visits here from time to time, and since he has already suggested that we might do something, I feel that this is a good opportunity to explore a very delightful piece of music. I'm really enjoying composing as the Pastorale takes shape. Beginning to play regularly for the Tuesday services – I do find these services so calming, and they tend to quieten me down somewhat – even if my faith has deserted me – and although I don't concentrate that much on what's being said, I find it is the atmosphere that affects me – so I'm not bothered about the religious side of things – at least I can let go in an explosion of sound if I feel the need, which happens quite often.

I really am feeling 'opened up' much more now that I'm using my creative talent in expressing myself through music – a lot is coming out as I write the Pastorale – it's showing in the music. This, in conjunction with writing this diary, is certainly stopping myself from hiding behind a shell of pretences and inhibitions.

Fuck it! – now I've had a letter from my wife this morning – crying again – angry – bloody guilty – why? – with all this other stuff I'm finding it all too much again – I'm exhausted with it all – started seeing shadows again – reliving the attack – hearing voices again – more panic attacks. I'm a fucking wreck.

Friday 13 October
Didn't sleep well, which is not surprising – but I'm hearing a lot of scratching sounds at night-time now – bits of crisps and chocolate all over the place – that'll teach me to keep food in the loose box – and hang it all there's paw marks on my diary – fucking cheek! – I'll have to lay a mouse-trap. Chatted with another guest about things and the trauma I'm going through and I mentioned that I wish I could put a lid on this 'can of worms'. He came back to me immediately and said he thought worms were quite spiritual. He mentioned how I was turning the soil over, preparing it for the future, and that I shouldn't forget that worms nurtured the soil too – without them the soil

would be nothing. So what I need to do is to change my attitude towards them, and see them in a positive light and see myself too in a positive light.

I am not, and never have been, happy with my perception of myself, which is the main reason why I've been putting on an act of being someone else for so long – ever since I was a child of round about six or seven – always living up to other people's expectations and other people's ideas of who I thought they wanted me to be. Now I've a chance to let me be made me. Now I'll go and do some bloody digging.

Later on. Laid a mouse trap! I keep on suffering from colds and flu, aches and pains etc. I'm sure it is something to do with the outward signs reflecting what is happening internally. As I dig in the garden my perception of nature is gradually changing, I feel. I'm noticing sounds that I haven't heard before – and I'm noticing colours, flowers, birds, etc. The countryside round here is so beautiful. I'm also noticing how I'm beginning to 'sense' as all this is happening – my senses are so much more alert than they ever have been, I think. I've been blocking out all this because my mind – my whole being – was concerned and taken over by so much stuff – maybe I'm beginning to see a little bit of light – don't know – but something is happening to me.

Finished composing the Pastorale – at least I think I have – it seems quite good to me – very expressive, which is not at all surprising! I have a sense that I'm beginning to balance things in my life at Pilsdon – a balance between being with people and being on my own. A balance between working and relaxing. A balance between resting and meditating.

Sunday 15 October
Still not sleeping well – maybe I should go and see the doctor. Anyway I did something a little gentler than digging and did some hoeing and weeding which made my back ache! Helped

Community worship in the church

to collate some 200 service sheets for the anniversary celebrations. Got some items from the pottery – some made by Andrew and some by another guest – for Christmas presents. Oh fuck it! I'm fifty this year – cancelled a party I'd planned for fifty friends and family earlier in August before I came to Pilsdon. It's what could have been which gets to me. Had some good games of snooker last night after supper and I really enjoyed the Service of Light in the chapel – OK maybe I do shed some tears during the course of it – but somehow I'm beginning to find it quite meaningful besides finding it being peaceful as I have mentioned before.

I believe it is Peter's birthday today. There will be celebrations at tea time I think. He's forty-nine this year apparently – a bit extraordinary for me in that I look to him as a father figure yet he's younger than me. I feel like a child; even like a baby who's just been born. Maybe it has something to do with my 'rebirth' – the beginning of the birth of my true self?

8.40 p.m. Had supper. Well, now the concert is over and it all went well. We didn't call it 'Pastorale' after all but called it 'Pastoral d'Amour' – it gave me a certain sense of achievement – and the 'Sicilienne' went well and the audience appreciated it and the whole concert. Feeling positive – bloody hell, that's a change! Wonder how long this'll last.

Wednesday 18 October
Morning. Sleeping a little better – a little less agitated and anxious as I'm now becoming used to the life here at Pilsdon. I also feel that I'm getting on well with the other residents and visitors. Maybe the concert and all the other stuff I've been doing is having some positive effect at last. I joined the choir some time ago now and as I'm getting to know the other choir members I look forward to choir practice now – which is on Wednesday evenings. Had an interesting conversation with

Anthony and Andrew over breakfast about memories of schooldays – the discipline etc. While I was digging again in the garden yesterday some music came to my mind of a setting of the Nunc Dimittis. I must put it down.

Later on in the evening. Completed page 1 and a bit of the Nunc – a setting I've decided for full choir and piano. It is not like the Pastorale at all – it's quiet and gentle and I shall continue with it despite Peter's comment at lunchtime after I told him what I was up to – which was that he thought the Nunc Dimittis should be loud and victorious and joyful all the way through! Last night was really nice in the sitting room – (they call it the common room) – the lights were dimmed – a log fire – and lovely company – so homely.

Today has been so dull and miserable and misty and drizzly – depressing. Made some tea for everybody this afternoon – I know it doesn't seem much, but it does make me feel wanted and needed somehow – appreciated – and I feel useful – don't remember having those feelings before.

Feeling OK at present as I write this. I seem to be contemplating a lot – in a pensive type of mood – thinking a lot about what's happened with me over the years. And now I'm thinking about what could have been etc. – missing friends over the years who have died.

Spent a bit of time on the Nunc – going well I feel – seems to be flowing; also composed an Agnus Dei in forty-five minutes! – suitable for rounds – based on the old Chinese pentatonic scale.

Thursday 19 October
After choir practice and after I wrote the above, I went to the sitting room (common room) and listened to a guest playing his guitar – quite spontaneous – a homely, cosy, warm atmosphere – relaxing and calming – a bit spiritual in a way.

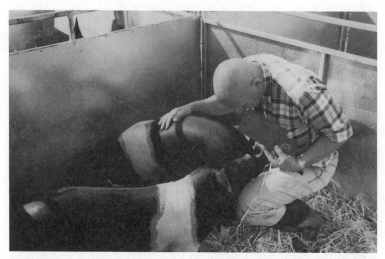

Prize-winning pigs

Some pigs were born during the night apparently – must go and have a look later. I've heard from my ex-employers wanting me to see them about something. Oh gosh! – or bloody hell would be nearer the mark! It means going up to London. Breaking up the journey and staying at my sister's overnight would be so helpful. Thinking about it seriously it really troubles me. How would I be on the train etc.? Panic attacks – voices – hallucinations – collapsing – Oh God!

Later. Finished the Nunc! – feel a sense of achievement – I wish I could feel like this all the time. Off to Crewkerne tomorrow to go to London and hopefully my ex-employers will foot the travelling bill. Spoke to my sister, and she is putting me up for the night in Farnham – feel better about that now – must do some packing.

Saturday 21 October
Well, I made it to my sister's OK – funny, I thought nothing of it – no panic attacks – no agitation – a bit nervous maybe but

otherwise OK. When I did eventually arrive I felt like a baby
of the family again and I really want to be back at Pilsdon. Had
a good discussion with my sister – I do love her lots – and
I am trying to look at the marriage (what there was of it) as a
complete mistake – I must try not to get so emotional about it,
but it is hard not to. We discussed divorce, or annulment
maybe, as the the marriage was not consumated. As soon as it's
all over the better for us both so we can get on with our lives.
My sister mentioned that she had been in touch with my wife
and found her suffering just as much as I was about the whole
thing. But there are no two ways about it, I feel really shitty
about it all.

Became nervous and agitated about going to London, so I
played the piano for a while and felt a bit easier about myself
and begin to feel settled in my sister's place. What an extraordinary thing it is to go through this process of being settled
in – never occurred to me before – all those years of taking so
much for granted.

Dreamt of being interviewed on *Desert Island Discs* by Sue
Lawley – a chance would be a fine thing.

Made it to London – I actually got there somehow – found
that I was being dismissed by my employers on health grounds.
Got back to my sister's – wept and broke down – listened to
some music of Percy Grainger that included a piece called 'The
Sussex Mummers Carol' – I played it over and over again –
think I'll arrange it for cello and piano – I believe it's already
been done, but not my way.

I really hated the journey to London and back – felt drained
and exhausted – just want to hibernate – can't bear this –
expected to put on a brave front etc. – can't – no strength left.
The journey was so stressful for me – and somehow the meeting, I felt, was dehumanizing. I suppose it was the state of
mind I am in that caused that feeling – I don't know – but I
did certainly want to strangle somebody.

Had a good chat with my nephew during the course of the evening – much in common about losses and attachments etc. – mood swings too – and he writes lyrics and composes songs too – some are really lovely, I feel – I'm proud of him. Now there's a good feeling.

Sunday 22 October

Pilsdon at fucking last. I'm back home – I feel at home here – did a little bit of a *Daily Telegraph* crossword and had a few games of snooker with someone who knew London well. Washed-up the supper things. Went to bed.

What happened this morning? I got up and nobody was around. Ah, clocks went back, so had a little lie-in.

Later. Arranged 'The Sussex Mummers Carol' for cello and piano as I wanted it arranged and felt quite good about it. Bloody hell, I'm so lucky to have this talent. Anthony said how nice it was to have me here at Pilsdon with the music etc. I must hang on to this lovely feeling – a really 'feel good' factor – feeling something of value as well as feeling needed – this is such a powerful feeling for me.

Gradually feeling calmer after the turmoil in London. Enjoyed a good music session after tea and attended the service at 6.30. Went to bed early – restless.

Wednesday 24 October

Went to the 7.30 a.m. service last Monday – finally made it there. Need to go to Bridport to do some shopping some time very soon. There are 100 wallflower plants hanging around somewhere waiting to be planted – I'll get stuck into that later.

I'm not too sure how I've felt over the last couple of days – a bit confused to say the least – feel a bit odd – suddenly I want to do everything at once or nothing at all. Feel as if the blood pressure is building up a bit. Even though it's bloody cold out-

The church and garden

side and in here in the loose box, I feel as if my face and the top of my head are boiling – the skin's becoming tight too around those areas. Headache – UGH.

Still no mouse in the trap – perhaps I'm doing it wrong – I'll have a word with Andrew. Ah, it's a rocker – so it needs to be tipped up on one corner – I'll try that and see what happens – hope it likes chocolate.

A new guest mentioned last night that he felt Pilsdon was like a piece of cotton wool – what the fuck he was on about I don't really know – he thought it protected people here from the real world outside. *Real*, he said. There's a lot coming to him in the future if he thinks that or believes it – maybe he's denying a lot – I don't know – maybe I should keep quiet and see how Pilsdon affects him if he'll let it. I'm going to leave this diary for the moment and come back to it later on ...

Later on. Planted the wallflowers – well, most of them – about twenty left to do – and I watered them – my back's killing me – and that's putting it mildly. Played the piano for a while –

but I do feel lethargic and despondent – at a low ebb – my GP's words – my words are .... and so on. I'm still restless and fidgety – so much difficulty in concentrating – bloody annoying.

However I do have a good sense of belonging and I'm making friends here. But somehow I feel as if I'm alone with everything – lonely – a feeling of isolation somehow – out in the cold – being punished for mistakes I've made in the past – "Go and stand in the corner," so the teacher said.

Another guest arrived to stay for a while – we met before during her short stay here and we seem to get on well. She asked me to play the piano after supper which I did – it felt quite a good evening to me – a long time since I felt as relaxed as that.

Oh God – now I get this feeling of being stunned – a bit of numbness – it's so painful for me to see things in black and white while I write this diary – it would be so easy to cross things out that I've written – but what I've written is true – so by crossing things out or by ignoring stuff I'd be lying to myself and denying things that happened. I feel really depressed now – more than ever before – it all so hurts so much – why me? – I suppose break-up of relationships do sometimes hurt and cause a lot of pain – maybe after writing this diary I'll begin to feel better – I just want some relief from all this stuff that's whirling around and around like some fucking carousel.

Later. I just wonder in actual fact if I was more in love with the idea of being married than with the person herself who I've known for some twenty-six years. Now there's a thing to say. I feel this has come to light because of the intensity of my inner desire to need to have that sense of belonging – to people – to places – it sounds rather a possessive attitude to have now I see it written down.

At some point on Tuesday – yesterday – I remember sitting down deep in thought, and gradually it occurred to me that I was still wearing the wedding ring – what the fuck. I just took it off and put it away just like that – no strong emotions – no anger – nothing vindictive – not revengeful – just felt nothing. I must try to keep myself in the realms of reality – it would be so easy for me in this state to fantasize and daydream.

Did more composing and went for a walk after tea with another guest – we shared lots about our thoughts on life in general – about our lives – and creativity – it all felt a bit spiritual in a way – it was lovely.

After supper last night there was a torrential storm – a raging downpour – could hardly see across the courtyard – it all seems to be reflecting the raging storm inside me. I wish I could be somewhat at peace with myself – the bloody voices, on and on and on and on. I wished they'd fuck off and leave me alone.

A thought just occurred to me. If only I could let God into my life even just a little bit, then just maybe a road to go down might be found which would be a help. I'm not really religious all that much – there have been times in my life when I've lost faith completely – but being here at Pilsdon in this glorious countryside, it's beginning to have an effect on me, and making me think about an 'essence of creation'. All that's happened to bring me here, and my experience in life, could be put to good use, if only I could see it all as a resource to fall back on so that I could help others.

Woke up this morning – that's like the beginning of some stupid calypso – feeling a bit dazed – and dizzy – it soon passed off though – and now I've discovered that the daziness, dizziness, and confusion could be caused by the side effects of the medication I'm on – brilliant – that's all I need. Went to my GP and swore just a little – we did talk things through and he's altered the medication to help me feel a bit more stable and to help deal with the voices and hallucinations. When I returned to

*A view of the church which I took from the garden path
early one October morning. It was used for the cover of
a new edition of* Pilsdon Morning *by Gaynor Smith.*

Pilsdon I felt somewhat fragile. Anyway I carried on digging, and a guest who knew that I was going through rather a lot to say the least came up to me and gave me a long hug – Christ that felt good – so warming – so understanding – nothing was said – nothing needed to be said – she really is a lovely person.

Began to think that I should give up smoking – it has been on the increase since I arrived here – and I feel like a cigarette right now while I write this. What is it about smoking? Is it just a habit or an addiction? Or is there some other underlying factor about it, like the inhaling being likened to drawing in one's emotions?

I keep on feeling that I want to curl up. I've noticed how much my shoulders have hunched up causing aches around my neck, so I've started doing some stretching exercises.

Saturday 28 October
Since Thursday I've felt agitated and restless, had indigestion and wept a lot – feel exhausted – want to run away – what from? – suicidal thoughts again – panic attacks – on Thursday I began to stiffen all over – had a temperature – sweating a lot and shaking – vomiting – queer feeling in the stomach. Mary suggested that I stay in bed – so I've stayed as ordered. Now then, reader, I'll tell you something. Since Thursday people have come to the loose box where I sleep and chatted to me, bringing things to drink etc. Wow, I felt like a king – it was so powerful for me to have people coming to see how I am – a really good feeling which hopefully I can hang on to for a while.

Everything inside me is like a whirlpool – whirling around and around – down and down – I thought this fucking medication was supposed to help these mood swings and stable me – like the fuck it has so far – ah, the doctor said, they might take some two weeks before they have an effect – brilliant. One minute I'm freezing, the next I'm sweating – some sort of manifestation – (how the hell can I think up a word like that

at a time like this) – of the suppressed pains and suffering –
(sexual abuse during the boarding school days etc.) – of the
inner turmoils manifesting themselves externally. Maybe some
of the pains that have been suppressed in the unconscious are
coming gradually to the conscious – AND – there's something
else too – it bloody hell is difficult and painful to admit that
I've dealt out as much pain and abuse as I have suffered.

Had a lovely long chat with Mary yesterday and she wondered if in addition to what I was going through maybe I was
being affected by the dynamics of living in a community –
there's a thought. I thought afterwards that maybe it is quite
natural for a person who finds it impossible to deal with internal conflicts and inner discontentments – maybe denying
them or even maybe completely unaware of them – can only
deal with them by projecting that stuff into or onto the community which then affects/effects the whole communal life – I
suppose it's bound to happen. Anyway, I'm feeling bloody
rotten, but to hell with it, I'm really enjoying being cared for
in such a lovely way – love in action – isn't that so powerful?
– all the members have come in to see me showing concern for
me – showing that they really care – Christian love in action
and just the prayer – in fact some of the residents too have
come in – it's really affecting me.

It's funny in a way that sometimes I get the urge to run
round the courtyard – round and round like that bloody
carousel – maybe I should – maybe it would help me to feel
better – running round in circles – acting out externally what's
going on internally. There's another thing while I'm in bed
feeling ill – and that is I'm being given so much opportunity
to do so much talking – and now it has occurred to me that
maybe I'm talking too much and that maybe I should do some
listening, create some sort of balance in my life here at Pilsdon.
Mary, bless her heart, made me some soup this evening, and I
must say it was absolutely lovely.

Monday 30 October
I seemed to have slept right through from Saturday till today. I did wake up occassionally to have something to drink, but otherwise I was in the Land of Nod. People who have come in this morning to see how I am, are saying that I look a bit better, and I think I feel a bit better. I got up to go to supper and received a lovely welcome from everyone – they were so obviously pleased to see me up and around again and better – supper had that extra feel-good factor about it.

Here we go again. Yes, I do feel better, BUT, I feel absolutely zilch – a zombie – numbed and confused. I'm at a loss – don't know which way to go. Finding it so difficult to concentrate and focus – everything seems cloudy – can't sense anything in particular – bits of feelings and bits of events in my life are flying around – don't feel grounded – fragile – just want to sleep – curl up – go back to mother's womb – feel safe there – emptiness – nothingness – just black – everything's black in a tunnel – waiting to be born – no light – stomach feels churned up. Is Pilsdon like a mother figure to me? Struggling to find the true self after all the acting I've done in the past. Where can I find the real me? Maybe when I begin to find out who I really am, maybe that's the rebirth – could be that's why I feel like I'm in a dark black tunnel.

Peter asked me if I'd like to take a rest from digging – thought I'd done enough – I think maybe I've done enough preparing the ground for the future – and Peter asked if I'd like to do some domestic chores. Ah, bliss – yes, Peter, of course. I said I thought I'd enjoy the change and that it seemed good to me – polishing woodwork, mopping the stone floors, hoovering, dusting etc. Would he like to see my shoulders – black and yellow and purple and bruised? Yes, I'd like the change very much indeed.

Thursday 2 November

I'm now sharing the loose box with another guest and luckily we seem to get on very well. We both seem able to open up to each other, taking turns to listen to each other.

The first morning I did the new chores I really made a pig's arse of mopping the stone floors. So I did it again later – properly. What the hell was I thinking about? I just don't know. However, later on, I felt that I was being trusted and relied upon – needed and cared for – such warm feelings to hang on to.

Feeling less tired now than I did – don't feel as if I'm just about to collapse. I can't say that I feel really refreshed – bright eyed and bushy tailed, raring to go – because I'm not. I don't think that I feel so emotionally exhausted as I did – there seems to be a feeling of an emptiness inside – a vacuum – which is rather difficult to describe. Maybe it could be something to do with the medication, or feeling a sense of loss – not only from the mental and emotional separation from the person one loves, but also the separation from the physical – even though sex did not play a part in our relationship, because I couldn't perform – maybe there's a sense of loss too from all that emotional and mental investment in the partnership to which I also had an attachment. However, maybe for me there's some sense of loss from being 'normal' … ouch.

Some of us went to Hilfield, the Franciscan Friary, yesterday. What a gorgeous place – such a calm atmosphere – it was a pity that the weather was so misty and drizzly, damp and cold. But still, as I write this, the place certainly touched me. I'd like to return there some time in the future. Towards the end of the day we all had a fish-and-chip supper and the energy levels, I felt, picked up quite a lot – it was a good day for me.

Had a conversation with a friend that lasted until the early hours – and found out that he was leaving with a couple of others – so there'll be a few changes – happens all the time –

comings and goings. We reflected on the side effects of medication, and how it can put things 'on hold' so to speak. If that's the case with me at present, then some part of me regrets that, but another part of me says, 'enjoy the rest'. There is a concern for me that comes up now, and that is what happens when the medication is reduced or changed – but that could be a long way ahead.

I was lent a pamphlet on the side effects of the medication that I was on. So here goes – nausea – trembling and shaking – sweating – insomnia – drowsiness – now I have a little bit of understanding of what's been happening to me since I started on the bloody stuff.

Seem to be making a better job of the chores now – and today is really beautiful. Apparently it's All Souls Day and I've been asked if I would play the piano for the service. And so I began to reflect upon the deaths of my parents, uncles, aunts, friends and more recently the suicides of people I knew very well indeed – people I cared for and loved. So I felt sad and was allowed to spend time contemplating, sitting on a bench which I moved from the garden to the meadow.

And so on top of everything that brought me to this state, is grieving for the people involved in those suicides – especially one – and just maybe I might write about her one day. Not now though.

Monday 6 November
Did some shopping – bought some things for the loose box to make it more homely and cosy – a 'lived-in' look. The walls seemed suddenly to appear so bare – so now it's changed – I think I'm quite pleased with the way it looks now.

When I returned from the shopping trip – (which went OK, but I did feel strong nervous pangs and felt that a panic attack could happen any moment, but it didn't, and felt very breathless and my heart seemed to be 'jumping' a lot) – I felt less

Two views of the manor house and meadow

anxious, and had a bit more energy, and less sicky and drowsy.

Had a variety of visitors – community members and some other residents – to look what I had done with the loose box and all seemed impressed with it. I do like the atmosphere now, and I think I've been successful in creating a homely feel to the place. Maybe it all has something to do with the starting of 'tidying up' the exterior before 'tidying up' the inner. I began in the garden, and now in the house, and now in the loose box. Hopefully, soon or whenever, I will be able to begin on myself. Looking at things in that light, things seem a bit hopeful for me.

Saturday was a lovely sunny day, and after the chores I helped get the bonfire ready for the fifth – bloody hell, there was cartloads of stuff in Pilsdon to put on the fire – it must have been at least twelve feet high, when Peter suggested we went with the horse box to pick up some brush wood – felt better having done some quite heavy-going physical work – especially it being out in the open – and it was good fun too.

After supper on Saturday, I found someone crying in the dining room – so I went to her and tried to listen with people coming and going. So we went to the house chapel where it was peaceful, and easier for me to focus on what she was saying. So life here is not about just me processing stuff, it's also about me caring for others.

Spent most of Sunday helping with the bonfire and later in the afternoon with the setting up of the fireworks with Anthony. I do like being out in the open – when it's nice – but it is damn cold. During the day, a guest remarked that she felt there was so much anger inside me – this really surprised me. I haven't noticed it at all during the last week at least – I thought my anger had calmed down a bit.

Went to the fireworks in the evening, and enjoyed the roasted chestnuts – felt good about the day, especially when a couple of wayfarers said they had appreciated my help with the bonfire.

The duck pond

This morning I feel less shaky and less anxious – a bit more settled – maybe my system is becoming used to the medication – and, more importantly, maybe I feel more settled having come to terms, more or less, with the marriage. I think I've found a way forward in order to deal with it, but I'm not too sure at present – it all needs thinking through – but at least it's a start.

It really is such a glorious day – blue skies and a little warmer. Before lunch I walked around the gardens chatting with a wayfarer – they certainly have plenty to tell about events in their lives. Then I attended the service at 12.45 in the chapel – it included readings from *Our Earth*, which contains a variety of writings and quotes from the many different cultures on our planet about how we treat this earth of ours and the environment. Although I've said 'this earth of ours', I believe that we are really stewards of it – and aren't we making a bit of a hash of it? Not here at Pilsdon, I hasten to add, thankfully.

When the weather is fine I'm spending time outside – I do

enjoy the chores though – it's a feeling of putting something back into the community, as I feel I've received so much from it.

Still I feel in this blackness – but somehow I feel my faith is growing stronger and that spirituality is beginning to develop. Now I come to think of it, my faith has really been in the material structure of the church – the institution – maybe now I'm being given the chance to see religion in a different light. I do have this very strong powerful sense of 'being' at one with nature, and I'm beginning to realize how healing it can be if one opens one's heart to it – and that 'healing' is spiritual in its own way, I think – and now I feel I'd like to make Dorset my home, and let the beauty around me inspire the creativity.

After supper I felt inspired – so with the help of Anthony, Mary and Peter, we altered the seating arrangements in the house chapel. So now the seats are in a circle – which to me feels not only less formal (because we have a church where there's a more formal setting) but a little warm and on the cosy side – feels more homely.

Had a lovely chat with Mary, who mentioned that I was looking so much better – had some colour in the cheeks – it really felt good to hear that.

Thursday 9 November
Morning. On Tuesday I began to hear voices again. When they start, they just go on and on and on – all about self-destruction. Do I have too much to cope with so that I should finish it all? Am I so unhappy in me being me at the present, that the only way out is to finish it? The voices seem to have a feminine quality about them. One is quite powerful and seems strong in the conviction that it is issuing a command which I must obey. Another voice is hysterical – highly pitched – and keeps on repeating, 'kill, kill, kill', on and on and on. Another voice is neither calm nor hysterical – it is as if it comes from a person

who is full of self-assurance – a strong personality and charisma, who copes with everything and the voice is quite deep for a female – a contralto type of pitch. But why female? Is there something about the voices which 'tune in' to an inner side of me that is female? Now then, while I'm writing this it has occurred to me that ever since I was a young kid, I have always felt much more comfortable in female company, and much more relaxed. I don't think I have ever been truly happy in male company – in fact, I don't think I have ever been truly happy being male. Christ, there's a statement. I've never cross-dressed and/or had the inclination to put on make-up. However, I did get a thrill dressing up as another person when I used to go on stage when I played for an Old Time Music Hall group called The Edwardians. That was acting as someone else, which I so much enjoyed, which had the effect of picking up a certain element of self-confidence, which really I don't think I've had much of whilst I was just me.

Now I feel agitated, shaky and nervous – which I should not be surprised at considering what I've just written. But memories of deaths are whirling around, especially the suicide of dear Alison, who I admit now that I loved and cared for very much – oh dear – I think I need a break from this.

Later. Everything seem's so black – mentally unstable. Why, oh why, isn't the medication working? I felt it was for a time.

Spent time tidying the loose box, and then played the piano in the church for a while – unusual for me, but it all sounded so clinical – no emotion came through at all – my playing is usually emotional – everything was in minor keys and very quiet, and that is also unusual for me – I seemed unsure of myself at the piano and also unsure of my relationship with it somehow. A thought crossed my mind just then – there seem to be so many discords and conflicts in life caused by our yearning for power – power in finance – power over material

things – power over people – power over nature – power of
possession. If we could only 'go with the flow', we would
create harmony quite naturally – going with the flow rather
than against it – going with the flow of natural tensions which
may bring about natural resolutions – living in harmony with
each other, with nature and Mother Earth. We all seem so
intent on our own manuscript, which bears no resemblance at
all to anybody else's – hence tensions and conflicts. That was
supposed to be a musical thought to ponder over.

I do so enjoy the Tuesday communion service – holding
hands at the Peace and during the Lord's Prayer – I don't
know, but somehow for me it encourages that feeling of a sense
of belonging – emotional for me, yet calm and peaceful. It is
because of that sense of calmness and peacefulness that I like
going to the services, not so much to do with my faith at
present.

My eyes are beginning to feel sore, and my stomach feels
funny – my muscles feel tired and ache – everything now

The church from the garden

seems such an effort. Some of me feels really cold – yet my head feels hot. My skin feels tight across my head – don't know what's going on.

I had a really useful chat with Peter after supper last night and he felt that I was trying to do too much, and that maybe I should take a short break, and have a rest which will do me good. So I'm going away this afternoon and returning on Monday afternoon. Peter also suggested that maybe we should meet up quite regularly for some short chats – to give him some idea what is going on with me – and that feels good to me. I really am looking forward to the rest – but I feel a little nervous about being elsewhere on my own. I do feel completely tired out – there's neither the motivation nor the inspiration.

After the chat with Peter I went to sit in the common room – which I tend to call the sitting room – and the lovely fire provoked some memories of childhood – like toasting bread over the fire at home, and marmite soldiers – cosy and warm. Then quite suddenly I became really disturbed as memories of the wedding came flooding back. It seemed strange – a strange experience – it was like watching a film. I didn't feel as if I was in it, but that it was happening to someone else – very strange. Perhaps it could be my way of trying in some way to distance myself from it all. A way of coping maybe.

Tuesday 14 November
Well, I'm back. I didn't take any writing materials with me – so, I had a good rest away from everything – it was a lovely break. I went to Sherborne, and spent some time in the peace of the Abbey, and went for some long walks. I met a rather nice person who owns a little shop selling coffees and teas, and, more importantly as far as I was concerned, sumptuous home-made lemon roulades – once I had three helpings during one sitting.

Alan picked me up from the station yesterday afternoon, and we had a really good conversation about life – thinking less and sensing more – making space and time for meditation and relaxation – we seemed to cover a lot of ground. When we arrived back at Pilsdon, I got such a lovely welcome. Both Mary and Anthony said, "Welcome home" – that was so nice, and other people too seemed pleased to see me back.

I found that I was sharing the loose box with another guest who was here on a short-term visit, and is looking forward to coming here for a longer period some time in the near future.

I find myself dwelling on the words "Welcome home" – I'm not too sure how I feel about that at the present time – Pilsdon being my home – I think I feel that I'm in some sort of transition – which is maybe why I still have an unsettling feeling, which could be compounding agitation and the whirling around inside me.

Whilst I was doing the chores I had a chat with Anthony who asked me if I would consider looking after the house chapel – which means polishing rather a lot of woodwork – floor, wall panelling, and chairs, table, and the window ledges – not forgetting some flower arrangements. I said that I thought it a lovely idea and that I'd enjoy it. So I'm doing that chore as well as the others.

Later on I needed to write a letter to my wife which I admit that I had been putting off – maybe because of the powerful feelings that it may have brought up. However, when I set about it, I didn't feel a thing – I just felt as if nothing was there. What was this scary feeling about? After supper I helped Mary with the washing-up, and went over to the craft room to join some others who were there. I enjoyed their company. I remember not so long ago that I wanted to be alone with my pains and hibernate. So now, maybe at present I don't feel the need to hide myself away – is there a change taking place?

Friday 17 November
Finding the chores hard going at present – aching all over – wanting to sleep and never wake up – how these moods change so quickly from positive to negative. I feel this time, that I'm going down into the depths – darkness – nothingness – just blackness – feel desperate again – don't want to carry on – I've had enough. Sweating a lot – headaches – not sleeping at all well – feel confused – can't concentrate – fucking voices again – agitated – feel that I not only want to slow down, but that I want to stop altogether – somehow it feels as if my system is at panic stations inside – hysterical – if only my inside would quieten down and give me space for relaxing.

There are, though, a couple of calming factors that are helping me at present besides the support and the warmth of friendships from the members and other guests. One is nature – the animals that are here at Pilsdon – sheep, cows, pigs, donkeys, goat, chickens, ducks and a lovely cat called Daisy – and also the countryside. Another calming factor is being in the house chapel more often – polishing the woodwork, and

Feeding time

Milking time

making the occasional flower arrangements.

But, something else is troubling me a bit and that is losing track of time and days – finding it difficult to remember things. My mouth seems like a birdcage. Blackness seems to be all around me – can't get rid of it. Nibbling a lot – comfort eating, I expect. The doctor says that I am becoming dehydrated – I am a person who sweats a lot anyway, but the medication makes it much worse, so I should be drinking loads of water every day – dehydration plays havoc with one's mental system, as well as one's physical. Not feeling well again – feeling sick.

Tuesday 21 November
Drinking loads of water, and now feel less sicky – feel a bit better in myself in fact. Enjoying the chores and feel less exhausted – even though I seem to be going to the loo rather a lot. I've been shopping again, and bought more things for the loose box, and it definitely looks more homely.

It has taken me a long time to adjust to this situation, and to this way of life. I've never before experienced the likes of Pilsdon – so this is quite a learning experience for me.

The weather is good, but it feels freezing to me – I'm just beginning to feel less desperate – things seem less black than they were – spending more time helping around the place after doing the chores, and more time being with others. I'm also beginning to sleep a little better.

There seems now to be less intensity inside me – feeling more relaxed now – don't feel at panic stations and in a state of hysteria – beginning to calm down a bit – not rushing into things as I was doing during the first couple of months here.

I'm now sharing the loose box with a guest who was here earlier this month – and we seem to get on well – what the bloody fuck will happen when I don't get on with someone sharing the loose box?

There seems to me to be a pattern that's forming – because it has occurred to me that when I get up in the morning I am at a low ebb – but later on in the day things tend to lighten somehow. Also, I feel that I keep on letting myself down – expecting too much of myself – "I've been here two months now, so be strong and brave … go." This attitude of mine only brings with it a sense of abusing the inner self – surely, can't I, after all this time, begin to learn that I can be kind to myself? I'm just continuing the pattern of self-abuse, learnt by the experiences of school life. Isn't it time for a change, for God's sake?

The medication could be helping to ease the intensity of things – but, it has to be said, just as importantly it is the people here at Pilsdon, especially the members, who are also helping.

It's happening to me so often now, that I seem to be in 'my own little world' – miles away. Is this a way of blocking things out which are too painful to face at the present time? While I'm in this state, it is only too apparent that I come over as being rude to other people – tending even to ignore them – I must try to pay them more attention.

Something is also going on with me which I don't think I've yet touched on, and that is that when I'm in a helpless state, a fragile state, feeling vulnerable, I tend to take on board other people's anger and discontentments which they project on to me, and in doing so it's all mixed up with my own stuff that's whirling around like that bloody carousel. No wonder I'm in the fucking state I'm in.

Monday 27 November
Well, I've now been here two months – it seems to have gone so quickly – and what is occurring to me is that although it is not all that long ago since I got married and had a home and a good job, it all seems so long ago – a decade – another world away.

If only I could discard other people's projections of discontentments, bitterness, and anger. I wish I could protect myself in some way. After all, I've so much of my own stuff to deal with.

I've begun to do an extra chore, in looking after the common room – which I still call the sitting room – and make up the fireplace. I do like building fires – the bigger the better.

Over the last few days, my mood swings have not been so exaggerated – I feel a little calmer and more settled within – more stable – I don't find myself in the depths so much at the present time.

I've thought about how we, sometimes, can be so hard on ourselves and blame God for it – when it is in actual fact only us being hard on ourselves. What God may be trying to do is, in actual fact, trying to 'soften' us up – so he can get through to us. Isn't it so common that in times of hardship we say that we can cope? – I'll go on being the big 'I am' rather than accept what's happened, and soften up, and ask for help. Don't we so often hide our true selves behind a fucking great big thick wall of make believe? And while I'm on my high horse, when was the last time I actually asked for help? I never have … I think I've suddenly fallen off the horse.

I went to a lovely place for a retreat, near the coast, called Othona. Peter led the retreat, and he asked me if I'd play the piano for some hymns. I met the core members of the community who put on special events throughout the year, with some breaks so people can go and 'just be'. I'd like to visit Othona again. I feel it has something rather special about it that's inspirational as well as spiritual.

I feel I am really beginning to be so affected by other people here at Pilsdon, and by the ethos and spirituality of the place. I don't feel I'm so much in my own little world with my traumas and troubles. I'm beginning to notice other people's behaviour and how they affect me and treat me. This is all very well – I do find it so easy to notice and express how I'm affected by others and situations – but am I so good at realizing and noticing how I affect others?

Friday 1 December
I'm beginning now to discover a little bit about myself and growing gradually in some understanding of who I really am. Amongst all the whirling around and traumas and changes in life, I believe a 'new' me is emerging. I'm not sure, but something's happening. All I know is, that basically I am a very shy person – very quiet, thoughtful, and meditative. However, there seems to be another side to my personality that doesn't mind being the centre of attention – taking centre stage, talking too much and trying to 'top' what other people have said – which usually has the effect of me finishing up making a fool of myself.

What I must try and do, and writing this diary is helping me, is to be honest with myself – not to deceive myself – to be

what is termed 'grounded' and not live in a fantasy world – to
be open to myself and others as far as I am able – to memories,
feelings, and emotions – to be open to others so that they can
'off load' if they want – and not shut myself off from everything and everyone.

There is inside me something which makes me strive for the
unattainable – yet in the event, when I am able to attain whatever it is, I seem to want to let it go, and do so. This has applied
so much to the relationships that I have had so far in my life,
with the result that if they remain unattainable I tend to fantasize about them, and so live in a totally unreal world.

Really enjoying the chores now, especially the house chapel
– I don't feel so exhausted at the present time, and I feel more
creative. My mood being on the stable side at present, is helping me an awful lot – it is so exhausting when the mood
swings are exaggerated – I have no energy left to do things.
I suppose things are not so black as they were – so that's good.
"THAT'S GOOD," I just said – bloody hell, I'd say it was fucking good.

I've heard about an Advent concert at Othona which is on
next Saturday so I've put my name down for it – really looking forward to that.

Feeling a sense of belonging here now.

There are times when I just feel, with all the whirling
around, that bits of me are flying around all over the place – it
is a peculiar feeling – difficult to describe – it's a feeling of
being disintegrated – in fact it sounds silly, but there are times
when I just don't feel as if I'm 'being' at all.

All this mental and emotional upset within me is making me
think that it would be wise and better for me, my brother and
sister, if I were to stay here at Pilsdon for Christmas. I've a
vague idea that I may find Christmas, and the New Year, this
year rather difficult to cope with.

Oh Christ, I thought the medication was helping me to feel

somewhat stable – but here we go again – still up and down like a fucking yo-yo. I feel despondent – low in spirits – again I feel I want to curl up and die.

Tuesday 5 December
More bad nights and suicidal thoughts – angry episodes – feel like killing someone, if not myself – things are really whirling around inside me now – all fucking mixed up – can't focus even on one thing – can't concentrate.

A respite from it all occurred when I went to the concert at Othona. It was absolutely lovely – very moving for me – it is such a lovely place with such a lovely atmosphere. I must come here again – and then fucking what – all of a sudden at the back of my mind something pulls me down like a shot.

Doing the chores every day OK – still tend to rush things though – if only I could calm down. Spending some of the afternoons in the vegetable gardens digging trenches. What is all this? My shoulders are still black and blue from the last onslaught in the gardens. What is all this about?

At present I'm going in one minute from being really angry to suddenly being tearful – sometimes I feel just like a baby. Then quite suddenly I feel nothing – totally numbed – really queer feeling like a robot inside. Then there are times when I feel so confused – in a real muddle.

Peter wondered if I would like to submit a format for the carol service this year – or to come up with some ideas anyway. I think I'd like to get stuck into that. Time to think about something else that really is important for the community, and divert my attention away from myself.

Saturday 9 December
Enjoying the time writing out ideas for the carol service, and I think I may have come up with a reasonable format and programme – I love looking through various books for suitable

readings and prayers to go with the carols that are being sung. I've been to see the GP again – examined my shoulders and upper armpits which are so bruised. Apparently I've torn some ligaments – so he's given me some pain killers – had an injection – and in no uncertain terms: "No digging." I was about to say 'pity', but the only word which fits in with my feelings at present, is 'bollocks'. I really love being outside, turning the soil over – being in the open air – I don't feel hemmed in then.

During the week I've been short tempered and irritable. I'm tired – not sleeping well at all. However, yesterday, I completed a draft of the carol service, which includes a few readings from the Bible, some poetry, prayers, and carols. Peter said that he liked it – sense of an achievement which immediately helped me to feel better about myself

I'm attending Compline more often – a service at 9 p.m. or thereabouts – towards the end of the day – and I do find it restful and peaceful and calming. I now feel that I am in a better frame of mind. I don't think it is just the services and/or being in the house chapel or the church. I do think it is a combination of things which includes those opportunities to be in the house chapel or church, the opportunity for creativity, the writing of this diary, the beautiful countryside, and more importantly the love, care, and support from the members and other guests who have become friends.

I've thought about the marriage, and I think it's time to try to put it behind me and go for an annulment. I'll do this in the new year and find a good local solicitor who can do it through legal aid.

Friday 15 December
I helped during the week, after doing the chores, with the mailing of some 1,000 newsletters and Christmas cards to those on the mailing list. I do enjoy things like this – anything to stop me thinking about myself, and also helping the

community – it's all very therapeutic. However, I do find it so difficult, still, to concentrate – and I'm finding my vision a little blurred – side effects of the medication.

Gradually I'm beginning to feel less anxious and less despondent – my moods are so much up and down all the bloody time – everything seems to have gone all haywire – and still all this whirling around.

Don't feel so much down in the depths of despair as I did; somehow I feel that perhaps there is some light at the end of this very dark tunnel – even amongst all this confusion – so that's very positive.

The guest who's sharing the loose box with me mentioned that I tend to neglect myself and that, maybe, I don't think very much of myself. He said that it would do no harm at all if I would look after myself a little bit better. So I asked him out-right if I smelt of BO and he said, yes. I'm not too sure what I felt after this conversation, but it did dawn on me how much he cared for me, and that it mattered to him how I looked after myself, and therefore how much he liked me – I began to appreciate him and what he had to say and told him so.

One thing that I find disheartening is the lack of communi-cation from so-called friends. I thought I had built up, over very many years, at least a handful of friends that were caring and supportive. I feel let down – and yes it does upset me. It is extraordinary, though, how much I came across this in my work with the mentally ill. Even close families would lose touch with their next of kin. Is it something to do with the stigma attached to mental illness? Is it perhaps, that some people are really scared meeting a person who they know is mentally ill, because it tends to reflect the madness that is in themselves? I don't know – we can make assumptions but everyone is different, and has their own reasons for their own behaviour. But at the end of it all, I think it sad that families, and/or friends, do not keep in touch in such circumstances.

Well, sod it – I've sent off a whole load of cards with Pilsdon's address on them, and we'll wait and see what happens. I do have a very loving and caring brother and sister who I am finding very supportive – this means such a lot to me.

Still there are times when I feel absolutely devastated. I really am having so much difficulty in letting go of the attachments I've made in my life, which either through deaths or separation now no longer exist – physically. I do tend to hang on to things – it is a possessive attitude to have, isn't it? – must try to do something about it if I can.

Suddenly I feel somewhat anxious about Christmas – I feel tearful.

Wednesday 20 December
Somehow, although I'm drinking lots of water, I still feel thirsty, and my skin has gone dry and flaky – side effect of the medication I guess.

Played the piano for Evensong last Sunday, and felt it went well – some people said they enjoyed the 'reflective bits' before and after the service. I tend to improvise quite a bit – my sight reading isn't all that good, so it saves stumbling over various pieces and making a bosh-up of them – and in any case, I haven't got any piano pieces with me at present, so just maybe, I might save up and get some from the music shop in Bridport.

I continue to do the chores OK – also helped with spring cleaning the sitting room (common room), and put up some Christmas decorations.

Finding myself very short-tempered – obviously angry inside – it's really unlike me – I don't think I've ever had a short fuse in the past – but I certainly do now.

I've received some redirected mail from my wife – no messages or notes from her at all – find that upsetting, and spoke to Mary about it all – it really is so good to have someone who listens so patiently. Maybe, as my sister said some time ago,

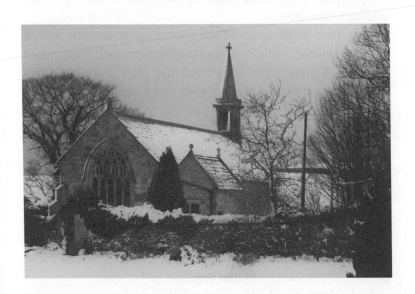

Pilsdon and the church in snow

my wife is suffering as much as I am about the situation, but I believe that I have tried to the best of my ability to smooth things over for her, and I've carried out her wishes without argument. I still seem to be at a loss with it all – IT FUCKING HURTS – just when I thought I had worked it all through – I obviously haven't – so I must try to be patient.

I loved decorating the church with greenery – had a feeling I went over the top a bit – especially when Peter came in to see how we were doing, and when he entered, uttered 'bloody hell' under his breath, hoping nobody heard it – but I did. Put up the tall candlesticks, and put some on the window sills, as well as round and on the altar. There should be in the region of just over two hundred candles. What a sight when they are all lit.

The guest who is sharing the room with me is going away for Christmas, so I shall be on my own in here I expect – we'll see. Pilsdon is expecting a lot of visitors over the Christmas and New Year period.

I've been thinking about the deaths again, and the friends who committed suicide – I'm not sure these will continue to surface and come to the foreground very often, but maybe they will once in a while. I just so wish that I could see them in a positive light, and see these events and relationships in my life in perspective and in context with the rest of my life.

People continue to come and go – but things are gradually building up for Christmas with a number of people coming to stay.

A few of us did a 'dummy run' lighting the candles in church – 275 candles in all took twelve minutes to light and were all snuffed out in four minutes. The church looked absolutely incredible – a fantastic sight. I wish I could be more positive about Christmas this year.

Well it's Wednesday night, 11.10 pm, and I can't sleep – the Carol Service is over. People came to me to say how much they enjoyed the service when they found out that I had created it.

I was so glad to see some people and friends from Othona there at the service – the whole evening, I thought, was lovely – one for the memory.

Now then, what do I feel now the service is over – I feel tired – but somehow I don't feel the heaviness – don't feel so low – the spirits have lifted a bit. Can't I hold on to these feelings?

Saturday 23 December
Today's my birthday – and I'm fifty – half century – what's happened to it all? I must admit that I can't feel too enthusiastic about being fifty.

Since last Wednesday, I've put on a bit of an act of being calm about things – I don't know why – when in actual fact, all is in a turmoil inside. I'm still not sure what this acting thing is about, but that's how I feel I want to be at present.

There are a few competitions happening over the Christmas and New Year period – chess, snooker, draughts, table tennis (which I've entered) – and I'm looking forward to that – a bit of fun.

I've been thinking about the relationship with my wife during the time that we were together. I don't remember paying her much attention – not listening enough etc., and maybe that I was not showing the enjoyment of the relationship – holding my feelings in – typical of me. No wonder we're separated. I should remember though, that 'it takes two to tango', and I should remember not to feel too guilty about it all and that it is 'we' who should share the responsibility, and the fact that she is silent with me, she is doing just that, and finding it just as difficult to deal with.

Suddenly I am aware of a funny taste in my mouth again – it has a metallic quality about it amongst what feels like a 'birdcage'.

Well, it's Saturday morning, and while I was cleaning the church, a message was brought to me that my wife had called.

Mixed feelings about that – still, I returned her call later on,
and got the answer machine – typical – we aren't in contact
with each other for what seems an eternity, and when we try to
get hold of each other the other's not there. Anthony, so
thoughtful, realized I was in a bit of a state and going through
a bit of a difficult time, came to the loose box and allowed me
to 'offload'. I don't know, but afterwards I somehow felt
'cleansed', and he certainly calmed me down an awful lot.

What a birthday tea-party – how lovely – it all nearly made
me cry – silly, isn't it? Had cards and pressies – and everyone
was so generous – it all meant such a lot to me.

I did some Christmas cards for some of the people that I've
got to know here, and of course for the members, in whose
cards I put a little message – each of them appropriate, I felt, to
that member. Some of them were quite moved by that – but I
felt that I needed to be real with them – I have such a lot to
thank them for.

Christmas celebrations

Thursday 28 December

Christmas is over, thank goodness – but I must admit I wonder what all those feelings and emotions were all about. The fun and the laughter, the superb meals, and the decorations, all made this Christmas time a sparkling diamond in a rubbish tip of black hell. I feel elated and spirits are uplifted. There were some sixty people sitting for the Christmas dinner – how the hell the members and helpers did it all I don't know. Fruit juice for starters, followed by turkey and stuffing with bread sauce, vegetables, sausage and bacon, followed by plum pudding, then cheese and biscuits. Jokes and stories followed, told mainly by the wayfarers, and some of us then took part in some games – very light-hearted – I found it all quite healing in a way.

Isn't it in my power to feel some pride in who I am? For God's sake, haven't I achieved so much since I've been here – taking a full part in doing the chores, and more – attending most daily services – being creative, especially with music; composing music for the anniversary concert and an Agnus Dei and Nunc Dimittis – what more could I expect of myself? I so enjoy doing myself down – doing myself badly – the more I abuse myself the better – UGH.

Well, having just written that, and having read through the diary so far, somehow I'm glad, and in some way privileged, that I am experiencing Pilsdon. For me, it is a big turn-around. I have few clothes and very few possessions – but, what the hell, what more could I want? At last I feel a particular sense of belonging that I haven't felt before – nothing too materialistic – more to do with human relationships – more to do with the relationship between myself and nature and creation – more to do with a spirituality that for so long I have ignored.

As I see it, my spiritual direction, at present, is about the 'family of Pilsdon'. I feel at home here now – now there's a statement – but it really is true – that's what I feel right now.

I look forward at some point in the future to being able

to be free of the internal traumas and attachments which are bothering me so much at the present time, in order that I may 'move on' and develop and grow as a being in my own right – a whole being. I just wonder if I can attain that. Writing about it, acknowledging it etc., is, I reckon, the first big step. If I have this 'yearning' to hold on to issues that are troubling me so much, and succumb to it – then I shall never be free. Spiritually I shall stay still and stagnate. If I can learn, somehow, to let go once and for all, then maybe I might just begin to appreciate myself a bit more. So, the first step in this direction, which I can take in the New Year, is to go for an annulment and finish any attachment that I may feel towards my wife. Once that is done I should feel it to be conclusive and to be the end of that matter, which has been bloody bugging me for so long.

The members are all supporting me in this action of mine, in fact Peter said to me that he admired my courage. Why the hell can't I hold on to the feeling that comes with that statement? When he said that, I felt a boost to my ego. I feel now, having just written that, and seeing it in black and white, a little better as a person. I have been seeing Peter regularly for short chats about the marriage breakdown and separation, and all the other issues that are whirling around. They are so beneficial, as are the chats that I have with the other members and guests that are here, who have become friends more than acquaintances.

Writing all this down, is helping me to see some light at the end of a very dark tunnel – it is also, I believe, something to do with the fact that I am having the courage to open myself up whilst I am here at Pilsdon, and in doing so, finding the real me – a rebirth. What I'm finding so helpful, besides all the other things that I talked about, is the fact that I am accepted totally, without judgements, without criticism, for who I am – accepted with 'warts and all'. Also, another statement which brought me to tears nearly, and which made me feel so good, was Mary saying to me that she was glad that I was here at Pilsdon – if that isn't a healing statement, then I don't know what is.

Although elated and uplifted, I do feel exhausted. Maybe writing this diary every day is one hell of a commitment, and it is very tiring too, and I think I should be aware of the mental strain it could cause. Also I should not forget that I am on a lot of medication – each medicine having its own side effects, and reading through the pamphlets it is no wonder that I am in a bit of a tizwas. I think that it would be wise to go and see my doctor early on in the New Year and talk things through sensibly, and see what I really do need in the way of medication to help me, and not to hinder me.

It has occurred to me how things might be if I didn't have any faith. There have been times in my life till now when 'performing' being a Christian was just a habit – a ritual – and when my faith was zilch. There have been times here at Pilsdon when I've felt like ending it all, and when faith seemed to have deserted me. But somehow, at the present time, I do not think that the issue of faith and/or belief, is, for me, of the utmost importance – for me, at present, what I think is the most important issue, is the one concerning relationships – with other people and with, as I have mentioned already, creation/nature. These relationships, I find, have a spiritual quality about them. You don't have to be a believer in any of the faiths in order to be touched by that quality. The non-Christians, non-believers, are just as adept at putting care into action – as I have experienced, and continue to experience.

My stomach and digestive system seem to be in a bad way – did I say seem? – they are in a fucking bad way – could be something to do with the nervous system, and the state I'm in. Anyway, what is so nice at present is that Daisy the cat has just called in as I write this diary on the morning of the 28th. Spent last evening and night with Daisy – very therapeutic and comforting. He really is a lovely cat – grey and white, and quite a character.

Tuesday 2 January 1996
Saying it's cold is a bloody understatement – it really is fucking freezing. A pipe has burst in the shower block, and we've
just heard that it is -20°C in Glasgow. What the temperature is
here, I've no idea, but all I know is that it *is* fucking cold.

Because of the digestive problems, my doctor has informed
me not to eat any dairy products. No dairy produce? Life isn't
worth living – the milk here is so gorgeous, and the cream ...
and the eggs ... and, and, and ... fuck it. The people who do
the preparation of the food and cook it, are now teasing me,
especially with regard to breakfasts which I love, especially the
home-made yogurt.

Had a really good chat with Peter about processing the
annulment. As we were talking about it, it occurred to me how
suddenly I felt that the wedding was a fiasco – in that it was a
publicity event in a way – and also how it had occurred to us
how we would do better career-wise if we were married.
However, that does not take away one iota of the feelings I felt
for her.

It's cold!

I'm still not sleeping well – lethargic – joints aching – trouble with the stomach – and Daisy the cat – (I have to say that because we have Daisy the goat too) – is in the loose box with me again – he's lovely. But all in all, I feel there is now less intensity in the whirling around within me, and that I'm becoming gradually relaxed a little bit – I reckon that's happened with the help of the beta blockers I'm taking. I still seem to have to remind myself to live in the world of reality and not in the world of make-believe.

Saturday 6 January
During the week I continued to feel the benefits of the beta blockers, and I feel much more relaxed – my muscles are not tensing up all the time as they used to and my breathing is noticeably better. Before, I used to tense up and, besides stiffening up all over, my breathing was rapid and I was getting out of breath so much. Now things are a little better physically for me – so now, hopefully, things might improve mentally.

I have been thinking during the week, about how long I might be here for but really, I know that I shall try to stay for as long as it takes me to feel strong enough to live outside Pilsdon.

I've just been asked if I would consider playing in a concert at Othona on 3 February. I think I'd like to do that – should give me something to work for – something to look forward to – something which should give me a real 'feel-good' factor.

My stomach seems to be settling down, and my digestive system feels better for having kept off dairy products, which I found so difficult, especially when I'm so tempted by the things the cooks come out with – such tempting creamy gorgeous puddings etc.

Some of us went to a pantomime – *The Owl and the Pussycat*. It was all very funny, especially the heckling from us Pilsdon folk. It was a really good-fun evening. Nice to get out.

I attended the Saturday evening candlelit service in the house chapel. I do find the service so lovely and calming, and warm and cosy. There's a stormy night outside tonight.

Wednesday 10 January
I feel that I am now beginning to feel someone of worth – I feel valued – I just wish I could have felt this before.

At present, I either collapse and sleep for hours and hours on end, or don't sleep at all. It would be so much help to me if I could attain a 'normal' sleeping pattern.

The friend who is sharing the loose box with me has returned from being away over the Christmas period, and has just said that he notices a change in me – that I seem much more relaxed. Maybe it is something to do with gradually being at peace, in that I am gradually coming to terms with what brought me here to Pilsdon in the first place. And maybe it is something to do with acceptance. But I must say that I don't feel at peace with myself. The pains and hurts are whirling around just as much as they were – and some more stuff is being brought to the surface, from the unconscious to the conscious mind regarding what happened at boarding school, and other stuff as well with regard to early childhood. I think also what is happening, is that Pilsdon is gradually helping me to put things in perspective.

I was asked if I would like to look after Daisy the cat – I readily agreed. He really is a lovely animal. I think it would be very therapeutic for me to look after him. I shall enjoy the relationship.

I had a letter from my wife this morning. This really upset me for a while, and then, quite suddenly, the feelings went – left me feeling rather numb – a nothingness. I wonder if that could be something to do with the medication? Or perhaps, something to do with how I am trying to come to terms with what happened? A mixture of both, I hazard a guess.

Sunday 14 January
Seem to be stable mentally at present, but I do have a funny, queer feeling of being 'robotic' in that I am finding it difficult to express my feelings outwardly. I can't seem to get in touch with my innermost feelings.

The cat's not been too well – digestive problems, I think. I spoke to Andy at some length about things and he seemed to understand what I was going through at present. I mentioned to him about Daisy, and he told me that the vet was coming to see a couple of farm animals, and that he would ask him to have a look at Daisy as well. Anyway, Daisy seems very sleepy now. He has been sick a lot, and suffers a lot from diarrhoea – funny, just like me.

Because I seem to be making some strong attachments while I'm here, when people leave after some two months or more, I'm really disturbed by it all. Two main feelings come up in me: one is envy – because I want to be the one that's ready to leave, and that I am really well enough to do so – and the other is to do with warm good wishes, hoping things will turn out well for them. It is sad, though, when they go – some sort of emptiness is left somehow.

There are times here at Pilsdon when things don't seem to go right, and people get on each other's nerves and scream at each other. One such morning occurred yesterday, and after lunch everyone seemed to disappear – where the hell they went I don't know, but after tea everyone seemed in good spirits and seemed relaxed. What caused the tension in the first place, I've no idea – but everyone was screaming at each other. I suppose it is quite natural, and part of community life, that everything can't be hunky-dory all the time, especially when people are living in close proximity to each other – tempers are bound to get short, and the fact that tensions come out in the open like this, I feel, is healthy.

Although Daisy is unwell, he is looking after himself, and

seems to be taking some pride in his appearance by washing thoroughly. Perhaps he's trying to tell me something. I think it is time that I took some pride in my appearance, and look after myself better than I do at present. Daisy is quite old I think – about thirteen or fourteen, so Mary has said.

Recently I seem to be spending time listening much more to other people, and taking less time thinking about myself and my problems etc. I've been to see my GP and feel a little better about things – although I must admit my physical state is getting me down, my mental state is getting me down, and my emotional state is getting me down. But I believe that I am at least a bit more stable than I was – or perhaps I am beginning to cope with things better than I was.

The vet has said that Daisy has a kidney infection, and the GP has informed me that I have a bowel infection besides other things, so we're making a great pair. I do so like looking after Daisy – he is such a lovely character – must be firm with him though with regard to his diet – so perhaps I should be firm with my diet too. I really believe that diet plays a very big part in how one feels about oneself at the end of the day. It can affect one physically, and so it can affect one mentally too. I know that one simple fact is this – loads of tea and coffee and high-energy foods make my mind work overtime, and leave me feeling bloated and lethargic. A good variety of foods, including fresh vegetables and fruit, can help one feel so much better about oneself, and working off loads of calories can help to keep one reasonably physically fit, and help to improve one's self-confidence and self-worth, and so improve one's appearance and one's mental state. When my mind is working overtime, voices and hallucinations disturb me incessantly. Caffeine is a stimulant, and I am finding that drinking more fresh water, and less tea and coffee, is helping a lot. The variety of food we get here at Pilsdon is tremendous – so I have no excuses now.

Othona have asked me if I'd like to include my Pastorale for cello and piano in a concert they are putting on. I'd like to, but I think I'll spend a little time revamping the composition.

One thing I must remember to do, and that is to take my medication when I should. I find it too easy to be forgetful and not bother.

Later. I continue to do the chores OK, and I've begun work on the Pastorale. Something I do like here, now, and that is the games of snooker I take part in, and the chats in the evenings after supper in the common room, which I still tend to call the sitting room.

During the week, it seems that Daisy has become a little better and, I believe, so have I. I feel really at home here now – this is such a warm feeling – a true sense of belonging. Also what is so therapeutic, is that I'm accepted as I am, with warts and all.

Daisy does not like my firm attitude with regard to the diet – but as he's getting better, he is becoming very affectionate towards me, and I'm finding that so lovely and comforting. He is making me think of him, and not think so much about myself. Also he is a catalyst for me to think about others in the community, and relate to them better than I have. Lots of people in the community are asking me how Daisy is, and then asking how I am – which leaves me no alternative really than to ask how they are.

I feel at long last that perhaps there is some light at the end of this dark, black tunnel that I find myself in – (sorry, English lovers – at the end of this dark, black tunnel in which I find myself) – gradually climbing out of an abyss. It's such a struggle though – the community is so helpful in all this. Thinking about this long, dark, black tunnel – maybe it is the fact that I am not only trying to come to terms with what has happened in my life, but that I am also gradually finding my true inner self – Pilsdon being some kind of influence to open me up so much, which also provides a safe place to do so – and not only that but maybe that Pilsdon is being 'a mother' in that it is gradually giving birth – I am being in the process of being reborn – so the tunnel could be described as being the uterus.

Tuesday 23 January
Good grief – now that's a bit of mild language – I have just received a little bit of money from my ex-employers – money in lieu of notice. With it I am going to buy a mini hi-fi, and some lovely CDs.

Gosh, it is so lovely to have some music in the loose box. I am on my own at present, so I shall have to watch it when I am sharing. I am, though, through all this, taking some pride in the place where I live and in particular the loose box. Maybe I can at last begin to try to transfer this attitude to myself – wonders will never cease – and maybe it won't happen just yet – but it must begin to happen soon, surely.

One of the things that I keep on doing, and which causes me lots of stress, is that I always leave things to the last moment before I get round to the 'doing', rather than the 'thinking'. It really does bug me, and I'm not too sure why I keep on doing it. It is something I've always done, ever since I was a child. Why I should go about things in such a way as to cause myself stress, I don't know – all know is, that if I could pace myself better and do things as they come to hand and do them at a leisurely pace, I would finish up doing those things much better than I do at present, and be much more relaxed about things.

The working of the Pastorale continues to go well – and I feel that I should have a sense of achievement – but I don't at present. All of a sudden, I feel so terribly low – it's as if someone's turned the light out. It's all dark again. The things that are at the forefront of my mind are the hurts and pains and the abuse I've done to others in my life. It's not as if I'm not sorry for them, because I am – I just can't seem to let go of them.

Garden chores

Daisy is such good company, especially now he looks so much better, and seems settled – I feel settled too.

Sunday 28 January
I've been thinking about having another weekend away. There's certainly a yearning that I have which is to run away from things; and I feel that this is something to do with it. There's masses of stuff that's still whirling around, which, it seems, I can't bear to deal with – but it's got to be faced some time. I'm not sure what it is that I'm scared of.

I seem to be enjoying lots of chats in the early hours with a couple of other residents, and it really is good, I feel – we care for one another. The two residents are male – this is such a turn-around for me – such a change – as before I came to Pilsdon, I only really chatted in depth with women, in whose company I feel so relaxed and comfortable. Male company drove me up the wall and made me agitated. I think I remember writing about this earlier on. Ever since I was a child, I always felt happier in women's company rather than men's. I have always felt, from as long ago as I can remember, being unhappy with my body, and always wondered what it would be like as a woman – not that I cross-dress, or feel that I'm gay in any way, because I'm not – maybe it is the fact that I have a strong female element within me. Anyway, I feel a little better about being in men's company now.

During the week, Anthony spoke with me at some length about what was going on in my life at present, and what was happening to me. This is an aspect of Pilsdon which I find so caring and helpful – it's so genuine, and helping me so much.

On Friday I went down with flu – felt really run down. Mary came to see me with a tray at lunchtime with some hot soup and bread, and she stayed for a while – that was so lovely.

Yesterday (Saturday) we held a barn dance – I felt so damn ill I couldn't go – but from the noise from the corner of the courtyard, people were having fun – sounded great.

Thursday 1 February

Still in bed – can't seem to shrug this flu off. One minute I feel better, then all of a sudden it comes back. Feeling restless and agitated. Staying in the loose box at present, and whilst in bed I'm continuing to work on the Pastorale.

Felt better at long last yesterday, and I completed the final workings and amendments to the Pastorale. I feel good about it, and feel better somehow now it's completed. Achievement – wow.

Got out of bed, and got stuck into some chores etc. – feeling much happier and better within myself now I'm doing something constructive for the community life.

At long last a friend is coming to see me to find out how I am, and is going to spend the weekend here – that's a tremendous relief for me because I've know him for some thirty years or more – I was beginning to think that he didn't want to know. Anyway, I look forward to seeing him again. As I have said before, I'm wondering what these so-called friends are all about, when they haven't even bothered to answer any of my letters or cards. Some of them have been friends for a long time. I must say that it does bother me somewhat, and makes me angry somehow, and on the other hand makes me feel that I'm not worth knowing. Maybe I should say to myself that they aren't worth knowing or maybe they have their own reasons for ignoring me, because they have problems themselves. Whatever the reason, it bugs me. Shit.

Thursday 8 February
The weekend went well, and so did the concert at Othona. The Pastorale went extremely well and received very warm applause.

It was *so* good to see my friend again. He had no idea what was really happening to me, and didn't seem to understand what brought me here to Pilsdon. After long chats and explanations, he seemed to feel for me, and really supported me as much as he could in what I was undertaking. So my spirits were uplifted somewhat by the weekend's events – in some way I feel now that a load has somehow lifted off my shoulders.

Thinking about the Pastorale and the performance by myself and the cellist, I believe we put a lot of emotion into it. It seemed to tell a tale of ups and downs, tensions and resolutions, and it reflected what I was going through at present, and also what I saw in the local countryside.

Last Monday I changed chores, and became the kitchen porter for the day. I thoroughly enjoyed it. What really helped, was the fact that the chef was in a fun mood – so we had quite a few laughs – a little healing in a way.

I don't think I've ever felt so cold – it's absolutely bloody freezing. And Daisy's upset with the weather.

At long last – I took the bull by the horns and found myself a really good solicitor to deal with the annulment. I feel at long last that if this process can be got through amicably and calmly, then we shall come out of it the better for the experience. What I really want to know is how much this is affecting me and my mental health. I'd like it to be over and done with so that I know where I am with the rest of the stuff that's whirling around.

Saturday 10 February
Since last Tuesday, I have been on an absolute downer. I feel exhausted with all this – working stuff through – chores and the writing of this diary. I just want to leave everything alone somehow. I've spoken lots about the things that I have done – but I haven't mentioned the things I haven't done – just a slight weakness of mine – and maybe I've talked at some length about the feelings that I'm readily in touch with, but not about the feelings I'm ignoring or denying.

I'm so fucking lethargic – I'm so good at abusing myself. I wish I could change this pattern of behaviour.

* * *

Jacob sheep

Wednesday 1 May
Why did I stop writing this diary? Maybe I needed a rest from it. Anyway, since I last wrote I have been suffering just as much as I ever was – even the inner pains and hurts are manifesting themselves in my muscles and joints – I'm really hurting all over now – every goddamn part of me.

I've asked Peter if he thought it a good idea if I was able to have an advocate/friend to help me through the rest of my time here. There seems to be so much to do. I have so much difficulty in focusing and concentrating on things, and I'm at a loss as to know where to bloody start.

Thursday 2 May
Met with Mike, my advocate, last night. I am so lucky to have such a good person as he is – so thoughtful and caring. He suggested that I wrote down all the things that I had to do and then he would visit me next Saturday to help me put those things in some order of importance – sounds good to me.

I continue to enjoy the kitchen porter's job – keeps me busy, and I like that – spending less time thinking about myself.

Had a really good meeting with the solicitor about the annulment, the progress of which is moving slowly. He suggested to me that because of the state of my health, it might be wise for me to consider giving someone Power of Attorney – a role which his administration department could fulfil. So I went for it and now I feel somewhat relieved. On the other hand I feel as if I'm losing control over all of my life.

I've not been to the choir since after Christmas – people here feel that I should return now.

I'm so glad I've started this journal again – but I must remember to take things gently, and be kind to myself.

Friday 3 May
I received a letter from my accountant who looked after my

affairs when I lived in London. It was so nice to hear from him. It really made my day.

Headaches are occurring regularly – and the pains in the muscles and joints are becoming worse – having some difficulty in playing the piano properly.

Everybody is telling me to ease up. I seem to be on the road to self-destruction ...

Feeling really sad this evening, saying 'Goodbye' to both Alan and Anthony. Both of them have been of so much help to me – I shall miss them. How I hate endings.

Sunday 12 May
Gradually, with Mike's help, I'm beginning to feel that I am getting on with some of the stuff – and paperwork – that I have to do – and I'm feeling somewhat relieved. It leaves me speechless, having someone like Mike who is prepared to help so much.

While preparing some vegetables the knife slipped and I've gone and fucking cut myself in the palm of my left hand.

Feeling so tired still – but I'm doing the chores OK, with some help because of my hand being bandaged. I've also finished composing an Agnus Dei which I photocopied and put on Peter's desk.

Seem to be coming down with a cold and flu – sod it. Anyway I made two saucepans of soup for the evening's supper today, which by some fluke or other, people enjoyed.

Pains in the stomach have started – feel drained, shattered, tired and exhausted. Thinking I might just get stuck into composing a folk mass. I've no idea why I should be thinking so creatively when I'm so fucking ill.

Thursday 16 May
Not at all well – me being a stupid arse, forgot to take the medication for a couple of days. Why am I so forgetful?

Played really well, considering, with the cellist at the Ascension Day service. Bringing up a lot of phlegm – it hurts – hospital appointment tomorrow at Dorchester. It's also very painful for me to go to the toilet. Everything's so fucking painful – it all seems that a load of badness is being brought to the surface – not only mentally, but physically too. I had no idea there was so much going on within me. At least I'm not 'holding it all in' now, so to speak. Maybe now I've learnt to give in to it all, and allowed it all to happen – maybe in some way I've even provoked it. I guess that in some way or other it could be looked upon as more self-abuse, but I believe this process or other that I'm going through can only have positive results. I really look forward to a rebirth of my true self – not being someone whom others expect me to be, or want me to be – and not putting on a fucking act, pretending to be someone that I'm not.

I think that now I will leave writing the diary for a while.

* * *

Fence-making

Monday 14 July
Very shaky – trembling – panic attacks – sweating profusely –
voices again – joints all stiff and painful still – people seem to
be getting at me – oh fuck, not paranoia.

Nights seem to be really difficult for me for some reason.
Voices getting at me saying that it's not worth carrying on.

Cut myself preparing salads.

Thursday 24 July
Feeling anxious – cold – sweating – very downhearted. But I
seem to be coping a little better when I'm out – feel more or
less in control of myself for the first time – that's odd, considering what's going on with me. Contemplating suicide again.
Headaches won't leave me alone. I feel so confused. It's so
good to have friends around who are so supportive. I really do
not think that I could cope with all this stuff unless I was here
at Pilsdon. It's just the right place for me. Now, this is the first
time that I've been in the right place at the right time. I've now
discovered that the sweating, shaking, headaches, breathless-
ness, aching joints, and the feeling of confusion, are all side
effects of the medication I'm on … isn't that just fucking great?

Now I'm going to stop writing this diary once and for all.

Broken Dreams

As children bring their broken toys
With tears for us to mend,
I brought my dreams to God
Because He was my friend.

But instead of leaving Him
In peace to work alone,
I hung around and tried to help
With ways that were my own.

At last I snatched them back and cried
"How could you be so slow?"
"My child," He said, "What could I do?
You never did let go."

EPILOGUE

Once the process of the annulment began, and I began to try to distance myself from my wife emotionally, I began to understand where I was at mentally and the illness I was suffering from. Up until this time, emotions regarding the split from my wife seemed to be at the forefront of things, and it was, in addition to all the other things that were going on, whirling around inside, which was why I found life so difficult.

It seems that at times an illness like this can block out the pains and hurts of reality, and when realizing with insight the true nature of the illness, this too can be very painful. Life, when this illness gradually came to be better, was extremely difficult to say the least. Anger and frustration, bitterness with regard to "Why should it happen to me?" etc., and realizing that I was taking the anger out on fellow residents and core members, all played a part in what I felt could be a deepening pit. In actual fact, of course, light was dawning.

Discovering the real me was certainly not easy. Ever since I was a child, I've tried to live up to other people's expectations of me, and tried to be the person they've wanted me to be, finding my true self totally 'lost'. A couple of times in my life I have tried to fly away from it all and gone away, being totally ruthless and destroying all the lovely friendships, and cutting off those who really loved and cared for me. In doing so I nearly destroyed myself and the lives of those around me. What was I flying away from? Maybe I was flying away from those people who became too close to me, who were finding the real me – maybe I was really scared to find out who I really was – maybe not – maybe I was acting out a 'Peter Pan' and just trying to fly – flying away from reality because the inner self didn't want to grow up. I was in some way so used to the pattern of behaviour I'd learnt when I was a kid, and didn't want to lose it because I felt safe with it – but it wasn't being the real me. Growing up can be a very painful process, but what led me to leave Pilsdon when I did I really don't know – if I had the time over again I would have waited much longer. Maybe I was trying to fly away again.

Of course, having made the decision to move on I stuck to my guns. This does not mean that I suddenly became well, because I didn't. Maybe, in actual fact, I became more weak and exhausted with the occasional bright bits. Around September 1996 when gradually, with lots of support and with input from the mental health team, I became a little bit better. The process was a long haul, but going through it enabled me to have a much greater understanding of myself, and I believe I became much more tolerant, patient, and caring as a person.

When thinking about moving on, I felt it important for me to have a bloody good reason for getting up in the mornings, and to have a really good reason for existing. I felt I would need something to live for, providing some meaning to my life. So, during that year of '96, during one of my stays at Hilfield Friary, I talked at some length with Brother Aidan and Brother Sam about everything that was going on with me, and they put it to me that perhaps I might think about becoming a Companion of St. Francis. I needed no more encouragement and said yes immediately.

And so it was that the day arrived for a little service when I would make some promises to do certain things each day and each week. Coincidentally, Bishop John Neale, the chairman of the trustees of Pilsdon, was visiting Hilfield that day, and so supported me during the service. It was a tremendous turning point for me I felt – especially as Bishop John had helped me so very much with his insight and strength of faith during some of my very blackest of periods.

In order to move on I wrote out a list of priorities of people to contact, e.g. my GP referred me to the Community Mental Health Team, and so began the visits by the Community Psychiatric Nurse. Secondly, I then came under the Consultant Psychiatrist – who took over from the GP the medication for my mental health care – the GP still looked after my physical care. After some considerable time I was then referred to the Magna Housing Association who put me on the waiting list for a flat in the village I wished to live in when I left Pilsdon. I eventually moved to Broadwindsor in April 1997.

I have to admit that this move was extremely frightening for me – the first time I really was going to live on my own and be on my own, and without a job. It was going into the unknown. However, I made it with a lot of support from the folks at Pilsdon and from the people in the sheltered accommodation where I moved to.

I soon found the village to be extremely supportive of me as I tried to begin to take some part in the village life. It must be said that I treasure so very much the supportive friendships I've made here in Broadwindsor.

I have now lived in Broadwindsor for over five years. I can say quite honestly that it really has not been at all easy. I have had some dreadful moments when I felt my life was collapsing around me. One of the most surprising things that hit me was that I found I could not go back to Pilsdon feeling ill – the only times I sense that I wish to visit Pilsdon are when I am feeling well. What that is all about I don't know, but there it is. However, on reflection, it may be something to do with the fact that when I feel ill, being with ill people reflects back to me the illness in myself, which leaves me feeling angry, bitter, frustrated, and in a disintegrated state. In the event of being ill and in the company of 'well people', I feel soothed somehow, which has its healing qualities.

When I'm ill, the mental state I'm in disintegrates me, and the medication I take tends to compound that disintegration by treating all the different bits inside me – that's how it seems. So in organizing my treatment I try to find things that deal with the whole person. Then I feel in control – which is important for me – when I'm ill I feel out of control.

It is important, I feel, to relate to the reader that at the time of writing it seems to me that each time the illness comes back, I feel it has grown in intensity – each time it comes back I feel it is happening more often – each time it comes back I feel it is worse than the last time. I can hear some people say, "Go to hospital." I really feel that this is not an option for me at present. I am trying to rebuild my life here in Broadwindsor. I feel, when I am well, more or less in control of things. I have spent time and energy working out a treatment plan for myself – I have invested all of myself in it. And now, maybe, when the illness seems really bad, the only option is suicide. There are times when I feel I've had enough. There are times when I feel completely drained. If I am to believe, in these times, that there is a God somewhere who loves me, then it is important for me during these dark times to keep that love circulating – it must not stop with me. I am able to love as much as the next person – I am able to give of myself as much as the next person – I am able to care as much as the next person. In rebuilding my life here in Broadwindsor I have set up things in such a way that there is nothing which stifles me – my friendships – my work with charity – my creativity – my spirituality (for what it is). All this would disappear if I went to hospital. All this would disappear if I took even more medication. And so, maybe, the only option left is to take that one last flight. However, just maybe, when I am more stable and stronger, and the true inner self has grown up, I will be able to take a flight back to the mother who gave birth to the real me, and give of myself completely without reservations, inhibitions or pretensions, mind, body and soul, to those who seek comfort in her.

About six months after I moved to Broadwindsor, I decided to help out as organist at various churches round about – still going to Pilsdon occasionally to play for a midday service on Tuesdays and the occasional Sunday evening service. I have to admit that this talent I have for music has helped enormously in lifting my self-confidence.

Having a car has helped me an awful lot in getting about – I realized when I moved into my flat that it would be so very easy to become a recluse – and if I did that then all the good work that was done at Pilsdon would be wasted, because I would soon be on a downward spiral.

Also at the time of writing, I admit I still have difficulties mentally, but I find that I am able to cope with them a bit better than I did before when I was at Pilsdon. I see the consultant regularly, as I do the nurse – and I also have a support worker who sees me once a week and is an absolute treasure.

Yes, I am lucky – I do know that many sufferers of mental health problems have not made it whilst trying to live in a city, town or village – I do know personally six people who have committed suicide because the difficulties were too much for them. Between the years of 1982 and 1995 I was a therapist in mental health; first, working for the Hampstead Health Authority in North London and then, secondly, for the Family Welfare Association. It is these deaths that play a lot on my mind, and I do find myself thinking of them very often.

I have a cat – Pusscat by name. When I left Pilsdon they gave me Daisy to look after, who was such a character – always knew when I wasn't well and would snuggle up to me, with his head on my shoulder. Regretfully he died of a stomach tumour in the following September after we moved in. I still miss him lots, of course, but Pusscat is growing up to be something also rather special and she is very therapeutic for me.

As I venture out in my car I have to say that this part of Dorset in which I live is absolutely beautiful – the countryside

*Daisy at Broadwindsor,
two months before he died*

is amazing – the colours vary from day to day depending on mist, cloud, the height of the sun etc. Maybe I shall stay here. What future there is for me, is here in Broadwindsor, which is quite close to Pilsdon, and I find I am able to visit Othona when I can, and likewise Hilfield. For those who know me, I would like to re-assure them that I do not intend to fly again, because I am finding that I am setting down roots – and there is now no reason for me to fly – but, when I'm ill, guess what, I want to fly.

Changes are taking place within me – but I've a feeling that I am able to let these changes take place because of the 'care *with* the community' rather than the philosophy of 'care *in* the community' – (my support worker's comment). I have a sense of being valued – and I feel wanted and needed – all these things in the past really seemed like a dream before I came to Pilsdon.

What I do find so very difficult, though, is keeping relationships going – I find it so easy to destroy them, yet so hard to build them up. I also find that I am extremely forgetful, and find myself writing everything down as reminders.

There are still times of very deep depression. In these times I find it so easy to neglect myself – more self-abuse. I feel that the loneliness I sense during these dark periods, and the fact that I go back to my lair and hide behind my little shell, leaves me out in the cold. I still become agitated and upset about it all, and I still suffer the suicidal thoughts, but there seems to be more of a balance – things are not so dark all of the time – there is some light and there is some lightness – in that when I feel really down and 'heavy' I hold my head down – and so when things are light I hold my head up. It is when I hold my head up that I notice people's faces, their eyes, how they express themselves. I also notice the countryside and the birds and animals etc.

I still have a lot to learn – about myself and about other people – about how I affect others and how others affect me – about coping with my situation and accepting it. Now there's a big word – accept; it's only six letters long, but is the biggest word in the dictionary.

What I feel is important in my life, is to have a reason to get up in the morning, and have some sort of meaning to my life – to have a routine. However, it must be said that it is, of course, my choice whether I stick to the routine or not. I also find it important to really look after the flat in which I live, and keep it clean. I found in my work, and I am finding out about myself now, that quite often the external things reflect the inner ones, so by looking after one's surroundings, one may begin to look after oneself – taking pride in one's surround-ings, then taking pride in oneself. Is that a sin? Surely, it is a necessity for our own well-being – and why not then feel some pride in one's friends and relationships – I really do feel we do ourselves down such a lot in this life.

It has recently come to my attention that I now feel some-what grateful for the illness that brought me to a place like Pilsdon. I think that Pilsdon provided me with a safe place to be, and, as importantly, a safe place for me to find me, and be me, while the illness really took effect, with a result of break-down – providing a setting and environment for a healing process to establish itself.

I recently reread the diary when the Revd Peter Barnett had written the Foreword and asked for my comments. It was a somewhat strange experience as it seemed as if it was written by somebody else – or at least, if written by me, I had written it a couple of decades ago. Everything about what I had written, and what was happening to me then, feels as if it was another world away.

In August 2001 I took someone round Pilsdon to show him what Pilsdon Community was like, and explained to him what life was like there. I was at long last able to do this without powerful emotions and feelings being stirred within me, and memories whirling around. I felt quite calm and relaxed about the whole thing. So now, maybe, I have at long last learnt to let go of those troublesome periods in my life which brought me to Pilsdon.

Somehow I feel as if my Pilsdon experience was the setting for a new chapter in my life, where a new life journey began. I remember saying to someone recently, that Pilsdon was such a change from what I had experienced before in my life. Up till then, I was embedded in London's concrete, or in other towns where my life was so materialistic. Now, I have found a road to go down – a journey – which feels more comfortable and more meaningful for me.

There is one thing that I feel I need to share with the reader and that is the fact that, having been through a rebirth, I find that my true personality and character are still growing. I feel very vulnerable while this is going on. Somehow there just seems a conflict, because in some ways I feel quite strong – having been through what I have, I feel that I could cope with almost anything that life throws at me – the life experience that I've lived through has given me more understanding of myself and others – but, and there is a big but, when feeling like a child again, I feel, in some respects, very weak and helpless. When I'm really ill mentally, I look inwards, not outwards, so I do not notice at all what is happening around me. I don't notice the beautiful countryside, take no notice of the weather, and above all I don't notice that there are people in my life here at Broadwindsor who really care for me. It all passes me by as if it wasn't there.

It is often the case that a sad child, in the effort not to cry over a lost childhood, will also lose his capacity to feel, which is why he can't tell what comes from inside or outside. Like Peter Pan in Kensington Gardens, he ends up asking someone's advice, for example that of a fairy, in order to know what is happening to him.

and:

One of the principal characteristics of flights is that the baby is marked for life by the nostalgic desire to be held in its mother's arms in the hope of reliving those strong sensations of the very beginning of life. All these departures are in fact desperate attempts at finding a second chance; especially when the feeling of 'being human' has not been established with sufficient force. Flights such as these are looked upon as great adventures, while in actual fact the eternal search for lost childhood is a real tragedy.

and:

There is always the temptation to go back to the original nest, the mother's womb …

KATHLEEN KELLEY-LAINÉ
Peter Pan: The Story of Lost Childhood

There are many analyses of child psychology and depression given by experts, which may help us to understand what is going on. However, to live with mental illness in any of its forms, may leave one thinking: What the hell is going on? I thought God loved me – why has he deserted me? Why has he given me this bloody thing to cope with? What sort of fucking life is this? Life is shit.

I have been as open as I can, in order to relate to the reader, and share with the reader, what it can be like suffering from a

mental illness. As I have said before, when I am ill I find it a
lonely experience. Although I know only too well that I should
go out and be with people and walk in the lovely countryside
around here, I feel bogged down, unable to move. I feel inca-
pacitated. It is one hell of a struggle to get up, and sometimes
to go out is a 'no no'. But something within me says fight it
and fight the voices which tell me to kill myself. It is the fight,
though, which brings out the aggressiveness in me. When I'm
ill I want to be soothed, treated gently, to bring out the gentle-
ness within me.

It is important for me to remember that whilst I'm ill, there
are people who really care for me. They are very special to me
– because I do know that mental illness can be looked upon
as something mysterious and can reflect a dormant madness
that may lie in the subconscious in most people, and therefore
it can be quite a frightening thing to try to meet on one's
journey in life.

A divine Spirit is there for all of us. That Spirit may not be
apparent at times, but being open, honest, and true with oneself and others, gives the divine Spirit a chance to enter our
being. If we close ourselves up in our own little world, the
Spirit has no chance of revealing itself to us. When suffering
from mental illness, it is only too natural to curl up into one's
own little world and environment, but then the walls close in
and things can become worse – taking a flight back to the
original nest, the mother's womb. When ill, or suffering from a
wound, an animal will hide in its lair until healing has taken
place. Although it is very difficult at times, I think it important
to be with people, especially those who care and love.

We all have a capacity to cause pain and hurt. We all have
a capacity to be aggressive and ruthless. We all have a capacity to care and love. We all have a capacity to show that care
and love. My heart not only goes out to those who don't feel
cared for and loved, it also goes out to those who feel that,

for one reason or another, they cannot show that care and love.

The exercise of writing this book has been a healing one for me, and whatever these pages do for others, they do for me even more so – especially in learning to accept myself as I am.

There was once a stonecutter, who was dissatisfied with himself and with his position in life.

One day, he passed a wealthy merchant's house, and through the open gateway, saw many fine possessions and important visitors. "How powerful that merchant must be," thought the stonecutter. He became very envious and wished that he could be like the merchant. Then he would no longer have to live the life of a mere stonecutter.

To his great surprise, he suddenly became the merchant, enjoying more luxuries and power than he had ever dreamed of, envied and detested by those less wealthy than himself. But soon a high official passed by, carried in a sedan chair, accompanied by attendants, and escorted by soldiers beating gongs. Everyone, no matter how wealthy, had to bow low before the procession. "How powerful that official is," he thought. "I wish I could be a high official."

Then he became the high official, carried everywhere in his embroidered sedan chair, feared and hated by the people all around, who had to bow down before him as he passed. It was a hot summer day, and the official felt very uncomfortable in the sticky sedan chair. He looked up at the sun. It shone proudly in the sky, unaffected by his presence. "How powerful the sun is," he thought. "I wish that I could be the sun."

Then he became the sun, shining fiercely down on everyone, scorching the fields, cursed by the farmers and labourers. But a huge black cloud moved between him and

the earth, so that his light could no longer shine on everyone below. "How powerful that storm cloud is," he thought.
"I wish that I could be a cloud."

Then he became the cloud, flooding the fields and vil-
lages, shouted at by everyone. But soon he found he was
being pushed away by some great force, and realized that it
was the wind. "How powerful it is," he thought. "I wish that
I could be the wind."

Then he became the wind, blowing tiles off the roofs of
houses, uprooting trees, hated and feared by all below him.
But after a while, he ran up against something that would
not move, no matter how forcefully he blew against it – a
huge, towering stone. "How powerful that stone is," he
thought. "I wish that I could be a stone."

Then he became the stone, more powerful than anything
else on earth. But as he stood there, he heard the sound of
a hammer pounding a chisel into the solid rock, and felt
himself being changed. "What could be more powerful than
I, the stone?" he thought. He looked down and saw far
below him the figure of a stonecutter.

BENJAMIN HOFF
The Tao of Pooh and The Te of Piglet

Whilst rereading what I have written, it has occurred to me that
my way of coping with the illness has been to fight it.
Psychologically, in doing that, I have been empowering the illness to entrench itself still further and deeper within me.

The following is the philosophy of care and treatment I
pursued with my patients and clients as a therapist in both
individual and group sessions. Anthony de Mello SJ (a Jesuit
priest, spiritual director, and psychotherapist) shared in his
Sadhana (*Sadhana* translates as 'spiritual life') renewal retreat
during March and April of 1987, just before he died:

Don't change ... Stay as you are ... Love yourselves as you
are. And change, if it is at all possible, will take place by
itself when and if it wants. Leave yourselves alone.

CARLOS VALLES SJ
Mastering Sadhana

As far as I am concerned, if only I could change the abuse
and the hate that I have of myself to love then maybe I would
give that a whirl. To me it is not about 'giving in' to the illness,
it is about 'acceptance' – that word again. Why can't I accept
myself as I am? I just don't know, because there are people here
who care for me and who love me and accept me totally for
who I am. I have got to try.

In loving and caring for others why can't I love and care for
myself too? It seems so frustrating not to be able to change this
pattern of behaviour. It seems so natural when depressed, or at
a low ebb in life, 'to do oneself badly' and make things worse,
rather than 'doing oneself goodly' and make things better.

I said at some point near the beginning, that I had found a
road to go down – a journey. It is not a question of finding the
answer to curing mental illness, it is about a *search* in the way
of coping with the illness – and there are many different ways.
What I have shared is one way of coping. It is now time for me
to treat myself in a good way, by caring more for others, caring
for the environment, and distracting myself from myself –
being more outward looking. Inward looking (introspection),
especially when one lives on one's own, can be very unhealthy
and can lead one to be a case of paranoia. It is outward looking that enables the divine Spirit to enter one's being – or
bring it out, because it is already there, isn't it?

At the time of writing, September 2001, I have decided to
see where I am mentally, and where I am at with the side effects
of the medication, and so with the help of the consultant
psychiatrist, GP, and community psychiatric nurse, I am coming

off medication very gradually, taking the last tablet on 30 December. I've a vague feeling, that I am in for a bit of a struggle, a long haul maybe, but I've an inner hunch that I will master this illness and not let it master me. I do not know what the year 2002 will bring – a nasty shock (or shocks) could be waiting for me – but I reckon I'll make it.

I have been asked by Jim Cotter to put on the computer disk what I have written for the publisher of this journal. It is now September 2002, and all I can say is that the illness has come back with vengeance. It is important for me to keep outward looking rather than inward looking, and try to the best of my ability to care for others. As I have said before, for me it is not about seeking a cure, but finding the best way for me to cope – and I'm finding it rather more difficult than before because of my lack of faith at the present time.

In spite of everything, including the illness, I consider myself a very lucky man indeed – and to be able to say that at this time in my life says it all. The experiences that come with the ability to love and care with the core of one's being – with the 'all' of oneself – will always be with me, wherever I am and whatever I am doing.

NIGEL CAPON
Broadwindsor, September 2002

Psalm 139

O Lord, you have searched me out and known me;
you know when I sit or when I stand,
you comprehend my thoughts long before.
You discern my path and the places where I rest;
you are acquainted with all my ways.
For there is not a word on my tongue;
but you, Lord, know it altogether.
You have encompassed me behind and before;
and have laid your hand upon me.
Such knowledge is too wonderful for me;
so high that I cannot endure it.

Where shall I go from your spirit;
or where shall I flee from your presence?
If I ascend into heaven you are there;
if I make my bed in the grave you are there also.
If I spread out my wings towards the morning;
or dwell in the uttermost parts of the sea,
even there your hand shall lead me;
and your right hand shall hold me.
If I say "Surely the darkness will cover me;
and the night will enclose me,"
the darkness is no darkness with you
but the night is as clear as the day;
the darkness and the light are both alike.

For you have created my inward parts;
you knit me together in my mother's womb.

I will praise you for you are feared;
fearful are your acts and wonderful your works.
You knew my soul and my bones were not hidden from you;
when I was formed in secret
and woven in the depths of the earth.
Your eyes saw my limbs when they were yet imperfect;
and in your book were all my members written;
day by day they were fashioned;
and not one was late in growing.
How deep are your thoughts to me, O God;
and how great is the sum of them.
Were I to count them they are more in number than the sand;
were I to come to the end I would still be with you.

If only I would slay the wicked, O God;
if only the men of blood would depart from me.
For they affront you by their evil;
and your enemies exalt themselves against you.
Do I not hate them, O Lord, that hate you;
do I not loathe those who rebel against you?
I hate them with a perfect hatred;
they have become enemies.
Search me out, O God, and know my heart;
put me to the proof and know my thoughts.
Look well lest there be any way of wickedness in me;
and lead me in the way that is everlasting.

Let Me Sit

Let me sit
    with my sadness.
Let me sit
    with thee.
Let me be healed
    of my badness.
Let me
    be made me.

ERNEST CHITTY
Belsize Park
10 March 1987